COOKING WITH
HERBS & SPICES

COOKING WITH HERBS & SPICES

Sallie Morris

IVY ✦ LEAF

CONTENTS

NOTES

All recipes serve four unless otherwise stated.
All spoon measurements are level.
All eggs are sizes 3, 4, 5 unless otherwise stated.
Preparation times given are an average calculated during recipe testing.
Metric and imperial measurements have been calculated separately.
Use one set of measurements only as they are not interchangeable.
Cooking times may vary slightly depending on the individual oven.
Dishes should be placed in the centre of the oven unless otherwise specified.
Always preheat the oven or grill to the specified temperature.

ACKNOWLEDGEMENTS

The publishers would like to thank the following company for its kindness
in supplying the herbs used in the photography for this book:
Brent Eleigh Gardens, Lavenham, Suffolk
We should also like to thank the following who were concerned in the preparation of the book:
Photographer Roger Phillips with stylist Lesley Richardson
Food prepared for photography by Mary Cadogan, Wendy Dines, Heather Lambert
and Sallie Morris
Step-by-step illustrations by Jim Robins

First published in 1983 by
Octopus Books Limited
part of Reed International Books

This edition published in 1992 by
Ivy Leaf
Michelin House
81 Fulham Road
London SW3 6RB

ISBN 0 86363 042 1

Printed in Hong Kong

INTRODUCTION

Herbs

For centuries a myriad of herbs have been used in medicine, food and in witchcraft. In medieval times no king, lord or abbot would be without his herb garden. These herbs were not grown for their beauty but used in cooking to mask the flavour of ageing meat and scattered liberally either fresh or dried in homes to sweeten the atmosphere.

A delightful booklet from Kew Gardens entitled "To please the outward senses" gives extracts from 16th and 17th century writings crediting some plants with supernatural or curative powers. For instance, some plants were more effective when collected, say, at full noon. Chives were thought to cause troublesome dreams. "Common sage", it says, "is singular good for the head and braine quickeneth the sences and memorie, strengtheneth the sinews, restoreth health to those that have the palsie".

In recent years the demand for natural products has led to a revival of interest in herbs.

Use fresh herbs generously. Dried have a more concentrated flavour and quantities should be reduced by a third when used in place of fresh.

List of Herbs

Bay leaf: the leaves are an indispensable part of a "bouquet garni". Make this with a collection of, for example, two bay leaves, a few sprigs each of parsley and thyme or marjoram, a few whole peppercorns and perhaps a clove of garlic, all tied up in a square of muslin with a long string, so that it can easily be removed from the casserole after cooking.

Basil: its evocative, rather clove-like smell spells out Mediterranean sunshine. Dried basil is no substitute for the real thing.

Caraway: the seeds have a distinctive flavour as everyone who has eaten a real goulash knows.

Chervil: beloved of the French and an essential ingredient in 'omelette fines herbes'. In fact, it complements parsley and tarragon to perfection, bringing out their flavours fully.

Chives: have a delicate onion flavour and are a great standby both for their flavour and as a garnish.

Dill: unbeatable as a garnish for fish. When fresh dill is not available, substitute **dill weed** not dill seed. Dill weed is the herb used in pickled cucumbers. Fresh dill loses its delicate flavour in cooking, so it is best added just before serving.

Fennel: fresh, feathery fennel looks similar to dill

but has a strong aniseed flavour. The root is delicious when finely chopped and added to a tomato or fish salad.

Ginger: fresh ginger is widely available. The root is called "a hand", because of its irregular tuber shape. Peel, preferably scrape, then chop finely or crush in a pestle and mortar before using. Some recipes suggest bruising the ginger. Scrape, then give a firm blow in a pestle and mortar or use the end of a rolling pin on a board. This helps release the juices during cooking, but the ginger can be removed before serving if liked.

The dried root is used extensively in pickling and will most certainly be one of the spices in the muslin bag when cooking chutney. It can also be bought ready ground.

Garlic: the whole garlic is a bulb and each section a clove. Apart from giving an extra dimension in flavour to any dish in which it is included, it also has health-giving properties, cleansing the blood and aiding the digestive system. A garlic press is a good investment. Just trim off the root, then squeeze the whole clove into whatever you are cooking and the skin can be lifted out of the press in one piece.

Horseradish: a root rather like a parsnip but with a powerful flavour and smell. Grate as required – it fast loses its pungency. Thin slices can be slowly dried in a low heat in the oven, then pounded and bottled for storage. It can be bought ready bottled and bottles of creamed horseradish as well as another, which includes beetroot, are also available.

Juniper berries: have a rather sweet pine-like flavour. The berries are usually crushed before adding to a dish, to release the full flavour. They can be tied in a muslin bag if you don't like the bits in a casserole. They are used in marinades for game and the flavour also blends well with most herbs.

Lemon grass (serai): clumps of this tall grass grow freely in tropical climates. The stems, which look like a miniature leek, are sold in some supermarkets and Chinese shops in bundles of three or four stems. Any left over from your recipe can be stored for 2-3 weeks in the salad box of the refrigerator or in the freezer as follows: trim off the stalk (you can also freeze that) and discard the small root, leaving the fleshy part, which is about 5-6 cm (2-2½ inch) long. Slice, then pound this or pass through a food processor. Use in the recipe as directed but if freezing, pack into small sealable containers and label with the number of stems. To bruise, use a pestle and mortar or rolling pin as for bruised ginger. Dried powdered lemon grass (serai or sereh) is also available. Buy it in small quantities. Strips of lemon rind can be used as a substitute but in no way measure up to the real thing.

Marjoram and Oregano: both members of the oregano family, marjoram is sweeter with a flower-like perfume. It is one of the most useful and popular herbs and can be grown in a pot in the kitchen throughout the winter. It loses its delicate flavour quickly in cooking, so it is best added just before serving.

Mint: spearmint is perhaps the most well known of the mint family, but does not go well with dishes which contain garlic.

Parsley: the universal garnish, best used when really freshly picked from the garden and in liberal quantities at that. Serve parsley sauce on grilled or baked fish, with ham, tongue, on broad beans or baby carrots. It is used in maître d'hôtel butter, creamy potato or parsnip soup.

Rosemary: known as the herb of remembrance, love and friendship. Try to grow a bush near the kitchen door. Place bruised sprigs under a joint of lamb or under mackerel before cooking. Use sparingly as the flavour can be overpowering. Rosemary is evergreen, so is available throughout the year and flourishes in a well-drained, sunny spot. It is sometimes used in a "bouquet garni" and in marinades for lamb and veal.

Sage: fresh sage has a strong, pronounced flavour: the dried variety very little. It was highly regarded in the past for its healing qualities, considered the cure for kidney complaints, consumption and coughs, as well as turning grey hair black. It marries well with rich foods, such as pork, goose, duck, in herby sausages and with calves' liver.

Savory: winter savory is sharper in flavour than the summer variety. It gives a lift to salads and is particularly good when sprinkled over buttered new peas or broad beans.

Sorrel: one of the spinach family with a tart flavour. It can be used raw in salads (tear the leaves, don't chop) or cooked as for spinach and puréed to serve with fish, veal or egg dishes and soups. It is used in the traditional green mayonnaise "sauce vert" to serve with baked or poached salmon or salmon trout.

Tarragon: one of the great herbs which will transform chicken into something special. Tarragon complements fish and egg dishes, looks pretty as a garnish and makes a delicious herb butter to serve with grilled veal, fish or chicken. It's a delicious addition to a mayonnaise dressing for fish, too.

Thyme: one of the basic ingredients in a "bouquet garni" and is particularly good when added to a robust beef or game casserole or marinade. It blends well with a variety of other herbs in sauces, stuffings and dumplings. Lemon thyme has a more delicate flavour and therefore complements chicken, veal and fish dishes.

Spices

For centuries travellers, explorers and pioneers risked life and limb to bring spices first to Arabia, then the Mediterranean and the markets of Europe. The Arabs held onto this trade for almost 1000 years. The Romans then monopolised the trade having discovered they could boat across to India following the monsoons. For centuries the trade between the East and Europe continued, then in the 1490s the race began to control India and the Spice Islands of the East.

In 1498, Portuguese explorers sailed eastwards and commandeered the spice trade from the Arabs. The Dutch took the trade in 1605, and by 1796 Britain had taken over almost all the Dutch interests. The cultivation of spices became more widespread, the price dropped and now we can enjoy spices from all over the world.

List of Spices

Allspice (pimento or Jamaica Pepper): so-called because it has a hint of cloves, nutmeg and cinnamon, although it is, in fact, a single spice.

Cardamom: small, triangular-shaped pods which contain tiny brown/black seeds. To remove these, use a pestle and mortar to crack the pod or squeeze it between the finger and thumb, then prise the pod open with the thumbnail. It gives a warm, pungent flavour to foods. In some dishes the pods are bruised or cracked but left whole.

Cayenne: not to be confused with paprika pepper, though they are all members of the large capsicum pepper family. Cayenne is a hot and pungent fine powder but not so harsh in flavour as chilli, which is usually a bit coarser in texture, too.

Chilli powder: a powerful blend of several species of small red peppers. Buy it in small quantities and use judiciously.

Whole chillies: finger-shaped red peppers can be bought fresh or dried. Treat these with great respect, especially the fresh variety. The green chunkier variety is sometimes milder but still treat it carefully in preparation. Open it up under running water to prevent the oils getting near eyes or lips. Be sure to wash your hands with soap and water after preparation. Wear rubber gloves during preparation if you prefer. The seeds are discarded as they are fiercely hot. Chop the flesh finely in a food processor or pound in a pestle and mortar before using in curries or hot, sweet and sour dishes. **Dried chillies** are left whole when used for pickling.

Cinnamon: spicy, sweet and fragrant. Thin shavings of bark are rolled into quills or cigar shapes and dried, the not-so-perfect shapes being ground and used extensively in baking.

Cloves: give a rich, warm aroma and, like cinnamon, have an antiseptic, numbing quality.

They are an important ingredient in curry making but should be used discreetly, as the flavour can become overpowering. Ground cloves are used a great deal in baking.

Coriander: tiny round seeds which, when dry-fried and crushed, give off a burnt orange peel fragrance. It is one of the principal ingredients in curry powder.

Fresh coriander leaves look rather like parsley; in fact the plant is often called Chinese parsley, but has its own special flavour.

Cumin: a pungent flavoured seed which looks similar to but is much smaller than fennel. It is essential in curry powders and used extensively in North African and Mexican dishes.

Fenugreek: an ingredient of nearly all curry powders. The seeds are yellow/brown. Dry-fry before grinding to bring out the flavour. It is not recommended for use with recipes other than for curried fish or meat.

Mustard seed: black and brown seeds used in curry powders. They are also used in pickling spice and in such pickles as piccalilli.

Nutmeg and mace: the nutmeg is the inner kernel of the nutmeg fruit. When ripe the fruit splits open like a chestnut revealing bright red arils; these are the mace which surround the nutmeg. The colour of the mace, when exposed to the air, becomes a deep orange colour. When the mace is removed the shell of the nut is cracked to remove the nutmeg. These pieces of mace are described as blades and have a similar but more delicate flavour than nutmeg.

Paprika: mild and spicy with a hint of sweetness and comes in varying shades from red to brown in colour. Use it liberally.

Peppercorns: pepper is one of the oldest and certainly the world's most important spice.

Poppy seeds: easily recognized by their slate-blue colour, nutlike flavour, often seen scattered like sesame seeds on breads and buns.

Saffron: the dried stigmas of the yellow crocus. It is essential for a genuine paella, in Italian risottos and osso bucco. It gives an exquisite flavour but is used in such minute quantities that its main purpose is to give its delicate yellow colour to food. To prepare, place a few strands of saffron into a cup. Pour over a little boiling water or stock. Leave to infuse, then strain and use the liquid. Turmeric is sometimes used as a substitute but neither the colour nor flavour is so subtle.

Sesame seeds: combine with a wide variety of foods. The seeds are sweet and are especially nutty after a slight roasting or frying.

Tamarind: gives an essential sourness to many dishes from South-East Asia and India. It can be bought in pulp or dried form, the latter looking like slices of dried apple. To use, see page 67.

Turmeric: has a rich, warm, distinctive smell and gives a strong yellow colour. It comes from the ginger family and is bought ready ground.

Other Special Ingredients

Balachan or blachan (fermented shrimp paste) This is one of the less attractive smelling, yet essential, ingredients in some South-East Asian dishes. It can be bought from specialist shops in a block, 300 g (11 oz) and is also known as terasi. A block of blachan will last for up to a year in a screw-top jar. Store in a cool place or refrigerator. To use, wrap the suggested quantity in a foil parcel and dry fry for 3-4 minutes. Unwrap and use according to the recipe.

Bean paste Fermented brown beans in a paste which are added to beef or pork stews and in some fish dishes. They are quite salty so taste before adding any extra salt.

Soy sauce This comes in two varieties. Light soy sauce is quite liquid, has a more delicate flavour and is the most common; dark soy sauce is more like treacle and imparts a stronger flavour.

Preparation of Special Ingredients

Coconut milk To make 300 ml (½ pint) coconut milk put 225 g (8 oz) unsweetened desiccated coconut with 450 ml (¾ pint) boiling water into a blender or food processor and blend for 20 seconds. Pour into a bowl and cool to blood heat. Strain the milk into a clean bowl. Squeeze the coconut firmly over the sieve to obtain the coconut milk. The coconut cream, like cream in milk, will float to the top on standing and is sometimes added to the recipe separately.

Creamed coconut This is sold in 200 g (7 oz) blocks, which eliminates all the above preparations for coconut milk. It is very rich, so for recipes requiring 300 ml (½ pint) coconut milk, use 100 g (4 oz) of the creamed coconut cut into small pieces, and mixed with just under 300 ml (½ pint) hot, not boiling, water. Use as for coconut milk. For a rich coconut cream use half the amount of water.

Dry-frying coconut Put a quantity of unsweetened desiccated coconut into a wok or a large frying pan over a medium heat. Turn over all the time until the coconut is dry, crisp and a rich golden brown. Do not be tempted to leave it, otherwise it will burn. Liquidize or process until the coconut becomes an oily paste. This acts as a thickening agent as well as adding colour and flavour.

Dry-frying spices Use a heavy-based frying pan. Heat gently for a minute or two before adding the whole spices, which should be turned all the time, until they give off a spicy aroma, about 2-3 minutes. Lift out and grind.

Roasting peanuts Place the shelled peanuts on a baking sheet in a preheated oven (200°C, 400°F, Gas Mark 6) for about 10 minutes. Shake the tray once or twice during roasting to make sure that the nuts are cooking evenly. Turn out on to a clean, dry teatowel. Fold up into a neat bundle and then rub vigorously to remove skins.

PUNGENT SPICES

GINGER CHICKEN

4 chicken breasts, about 750 g (1½ lb), boned and cut into
 finger size pieces
1 teaspoon sugar
salt
freshly ground black pepper
7.5-10 cm (3-4 inch) piece of fresh ginger, scraped and
 finely sliced
4 tablespoons sesame oil
85-120 ml (3-4 fl oz) water
100 g (4 oz) button mushrooms, rinsed and dried
2 tablespoons brandy
2 teaspoons cornflour blended with 3 tablespoons water
1 teaspoon soy sauce
fresh coriander leaves, to garnish

Preparation time: 15 minutes, plus standing
Cooking time: 15 minutes

Use a wok for cooking this or a generous sized frying
pan. Despite the unusual amount of ginger, the flavour
goes beautifully with the chicken and mushrooms and
does not predominate.

1. Sprinkle the chicken with the sugar and leave to
stand for 20-30 minutes, this helps to release the
juices. Then add the salt and pepper.
2. Fry the ginger slices in sesame oil without browning. Add the chicken pieces to the pan and cook for
approximately 3 minutes. Stir in the water and
mushrooms. Cover and cook for a further 5 minutes,
until the chicken is tender.
3. Add the brandy, cornflour paste and soy sauce.
Bring to the boil, stirring constantly until the sauce
thickens. Taste and adjust the seasoning.
4. Arrange on a hot serving plate and garnish with the
coriander leaves.

Variation:
Use 450 g (1 lb) frozen Queen scallops which must
be completely thawed. Take care not to overcook the
scallops. Test with a skewer during the 5 minutes'
cooking.

CHILLI CHICKEN

4 chicken breasts, about 750 g (1½ lb), boned and skinned
1 teaspoon sugar
3-6 fresh red chillis
2 shelled macadamia nuts or 4 shelled almonds
1 stem lemon grass, trimmed and sliced
1 teaspoon fenugreek
2.5 cm (1 inch) piece of fresh ginger, scraped
6 small red onions or shallots, peeled and sliced
4 garlic cloves, peeled and crushed
4 tablespoons oil
150 ml (¼ pint) water
salt
slivers of spring onion, to garnish

Preparation time: 25 minutes
Cooking time: 10 minutes

It is important to use red not green chillis for their
colour.

1. Cut each of the chicken breasts lengthways into 8
pieces and sprinkle with sugar.
2. Pound or blend the prepared chillis with the nuts,
lemon grass, fenugreek and half the ginger. Transfer to
a small bowl.
3. Pound or blend the remaining ginger with the
onions and garlic in the same way.
4. Heat the oil in a deep frying pan or wok and fry the
spice mixture for 1-2 minutes. Add the onion mixture
and fry for a further 1-2 minutes, stirring constantly.
5. Add the chicken pieces turning in the sauce until
well coated. Add the water and salt to taste. Cover and
cook gently for 5 minutes.
6. Transfer to a hot serving dish and garnish with
slivers of spring onion.

From the top, clockwise: Chilli chicken; dried chillies; fenugreek;
root ginger; lemon grass; Ginger chicken; macadamia nuts

PORK LEG STEW CHINESE STYLE

1.75 kg (4 lb) pig's trotters, cut into 4 cm (1½ inch) chunks
6 fresh red chillis, deseeded, or 2-3 teaspoons chilli powder
3 medium onions, peeled
6 garlic cloves, peeled
1 tablespoon tamarind pulp or 6 pieces dried tamarind
   soaked in 150 ml (¼ pint) warm water (page 67)
6-8 tablespoons oil
2 tablespoons bean paste
2 tablespoons dark soy sauce
2 tablespoons light soy sauce
2 teaspoons sugar
450 ml (¾ pint) water
salt
fresh coriander or parsley, to garnish

Preparation time: 40 minutes
Cooking time: 2 hours, plus reheating
Oven: 160°C, 325°F, Gas Mark 3

You may have to order the trotters in advance – ask for meaty ones and have them cut into chunky pieces. There is quite a lot of bone so you will need this quantity for 4 good helpings.

This recipe is even better when cooked a day ahead. Remove any excess fat from the surface before reheating gently but thoroughly.

1. Wipe the trotters and set on one side.
2. Prepare the chillis. Cut a few fine rings and reserve for garnish. Combine the remainder with the onions and garlic and blend to a fine paste. If using chilli powder, then add to the onion and garlic paste at this stage.
3. Mix the tamarind pulp or dried tamarind with the water and drain well, discarding the seeds and fibre or tamarind slices. Reserve the liquid.
4. Fry the chilli paste in hot oil without browning for 2-3 minutes. Stir in the bean paste.
5. Add the pieces of meat, turning well so that they are coated with the chilli mixture.
6. Stir in the tamarind juice, soy sauces, sugar and water. Season with salt. Cover and cook over a gentle heat for 2 hours or until tender. Cool, then chill overnight.
7. Skim and reheat in a covered casserole in the preheated oven for about ¾-1 hour.
8. Serve in a hot dish, sprinkled with the reserved chilli and fresh coriander or chopped parsley.

CHILLI CRABS

2 medium crabs, about 750 g (1½-1¾ lb) each, cooked
2.5 cm (1 inch) piece of fresh ginger, scraped and chopped
2-3 garlic cloves, peeled and crushed
1-2 fresh red chillis, deseeded and finely chopped or 1-2
   teaspoons chilli sauce
6 tablespoons oil
175 ml (6 fl oz) tomato ketchup
25 g (1 oz) soft brown sugar
1 tablespoon light soy sauce
salt
120 ml (4 fl oz) boiling water

Preparation time: 25 minutes
Cooking time: 8-10 minutes

In Malaysia and Singapore these crabs are eaten in the fingers. Have some disposable napkins to hand and a large bowl for the shells.

1. Twist off the large claws and turn the crab on its back with its head facing away. Using the thumbs, push the body containing the small legs upwards from beneath the flap and separate the body from the main shell. Put to one side. Discard the sac lying at the top of the big shell and any green matter and grey spongy lungs known as "dead men's fingers".
2. Using a teaspoon, scrape all the brown creamy meat from the large shell into a small bowl.
3. Twist the legs from the body. Cut the body section in half. Crack the large claws and small legs using nutcrackers, a hammer or the blunt edge of a cleaver.
4. Gently fry the ginger, garlic and chillis (if using) in the oil in a wok or large pan without browning.
5. Add the ketchup (and chilli sauce, if using), sugar, soy sauce and salt.
6. When hot, stir the crab pieces, brown meat and water into the sauce and cook over a high heat until heated through.
7. Transfer to a hot serving dish or serve straight from the wok. Serve with freshly boiled rice or crusty bread and chunky pieces of cucumber.

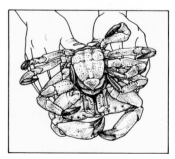 

Separating the body from the main shell

Dead men's fingers

From the back left, clockwise: Ketchup fish;
Pork leg stew Chinese style; Chilli crabs

KETCHUP FISH

Serves 2
500 g (1¼ lb) sole or plaice, gutted but left whole
salt
freshly ground black pepper
1-2 tablespoons oil
2.5 cm (1 inch) piece of fresh ginger, scraped and shredded
Sauce:
2 shallots or small onions, peeled and sliced
2 tablespoons oil
1 tablespoon oyster sauce
1 tablespoon light soy sauce
1 tablespoon sesame oil
To garnish:
curls of spring onion (page 18)
sprigs of coriander

Preparation time: 15 minutes
Cooking time: 25-30 minutes
Oven: 190°C, 375°F, Gas Mark 5

Ketchup is a general term for a sauce made from tomatoes, mushrooms, walnuts, or, as in this recipe, shallots mixed with Chinese condiments and oils.

1. Wash the fish and wipe dry with paper towels. Using a sharp knife, make 2 diagonal slashes on each side of the fish and rub with salt and pepper. Line a steamer for the wok with foil to retain the juices. Brush the fish with oil, scatter over the ginger. Cover and steam for 25-30 minutes. Alternatively, bake the fish in a buttered dish in a pre-heated oven for 30 minutes.
2. Fry the shallots or onions in the oil. Pour the juices from the foil tray or baking dish into the pan. Add the oyster sauce, soy sauce and sesame oil. Taste and adjust the seasoning.
3. Transfer the fish to a hot serving dish and pour over the sauce.
4. Garnish with curls of spring onion and sprigs of coriander.

JAVANESE PICNIC CHICKEN

4 chicken quarters, about 1.5 kg (3 lb) chicken, quartered
2 teaspoons sugar
225 g (8 oz) desiccated coconut
550 ml (just under 1 pint) boiling water
2 teaspoons coriander seeds
1 teaspoon chilli powder
1 teaspoon ground turmeric
1 teaspoon salt
4 tablespoons oil
1 medium onion, peeled and finely chopped
1 garlic clove, peeled and finely chopped
2.5 cm (1 inch) piece of fresh ginger, scraped and finely
   chopped
1 stem lemon grass, trimmed (discard root) and bruised
25 g (1 oz) flour
oil, for deep frying
To serve:
wedges of lemon
chunks of cucumber

**Preparation time: 40 minutes, plus cooling
Cooking time: 40-50 minutes**

Cook the chicken a day ahead in the spicy sauce. Drain
well then deep fry and take to the picnic. As an
alternative to making your own coconut milk, you
could use coconut cream.

1. Wipe the chicken with paper towels. Sprinkle with
the sugar and set aside.
2. Meanwhile place the coconut and water in a food
processor or blender for 20 seconds. Strain the mixture
through a sieve into a large mixing bowl. Press the
mixture in the sieve with a wooden spoon to extract
as much liquid as possible. Measure approximately
450 ml (¾ pint) of the coconut milk into a jug.
3. Pound or grind the coriander seeds. Add to the
chilli powder, turmeric and salt and mix to a smooth
paste with a little of the coconut milk.
4. Heat the oil in a deep frying pan or wok and fry the
onion, garlic and ginger for 1-2 minutes.
5. Stir in the blended spices and coconut milk. Bring
to the boil, then add the chicken pieces and stem of
lemon grass. Cover and cook over a gentle heat for
35-45 minutes until tender.
6. Transfer to a covered container and cool. Chill in
the refrigerator or stand in a cool place overnight.
7. Lift the chicken pieces from the sauce and drain on
paper towels. Dust lightly with the flour. Deep fry in
oil heated to 185°C, 360°F for 6-8 minutes until crisp
and golden.
8. Take on a picnic garnished with wedges of lemon to
squeeze over the chicken and chunks of cucumber.

From the top: root ginger; Javanese picnic chicken;
dried chillies; Fish moolie; shallots; garlic; Mulligatawny soup

FISH MOOLIE

500 g (1¼ lb) monkfish or halibut (or any other firm
    textured fish), filleted, skinned and cut into 2.5 cm
    (1 inch) cubes
salt
350 g (12 oz) desiccated coconut
750 ml (1¼ pints) water
6 shallots or small onions, peeled
6 whole almonds, blanched
2-3 garlic cloves, peeled
2.5 cm (1 inch) piece of fresh ginger, scraped and sliced
2 stems lemon grass, trim and discard root
2-3 teaspoons turmeric powder
3 tablespoons oil
1-3 fresh chillis, deseeded and finely sliced
sprigs of parsley or coriander, to garnish

Preparation time: 30 minutes
Cooking time: 10 minutes

This is a popular South East Asian fish curry in a
coconut sauce which is truly delicious. It is important
to choose a firm textured fish so that the pieces remain
whole in the brief cooking. The thickening of the sauce
is unusual. Some of the coconut is dry fried then reduced to a paste.

1. Sprinkle the fish liberally with salt.
2. Place 50 g (2 oz) of the desiccated coconut in a
heavy-based frying pan or wok and heat until golden
and crisp, turning constantly to prevent burning. This
will take several minutes. Blend or pound until the
coconut appears oily, then transfer to a bowl and reserve.
3. Make coconut milk with the remaining coconut and
boiling water as described on page 9. When the cream
rises to the top of the coconut milk, spoon off
50 ml (2 fl oz) and reserve.
4. Pound or blend the onions, almonds, garlic, ginger
and 6 cm (2½ inch) from the root end of the lemon
grass stems (reserve the remainder) to make a paste.
Add the turmeric powder.
5. Fry this pounded mixture in hot oil for a few
minutes but do not allow to brown. Add the coconut milk, stirring constantly as it comes to the boil to
prevent curdling.
6. Add the cubes of fish, most of the shredded chilli
and the stems of lemon grass and cook for 3-4 minutes.
Stir in the pounded coconut, moistened with some
of the sauce if necessary and cook for a further 2-3
minutes. Do not overcook the fish.
7. Taste and adjust the seasoning and stir in the coconut cream just before serving. Remove the stems of
lemon grass. Transfer to a hot serving dish and sprinkle with the remaining chilli. Garnish with parsley or
coriander and serve with rice.

MULLIGATAWNY SOUP

Serves 6
450 g (1 lb) shin of beef, cut into 2.5 cm (1 inch) cubes
1 kg (2 lb) beef bones, washed
about 2.25 litres (4 pints) water
1 tablespoon coriander seeds
½ teaspoon black peppercorns
2 teaspoons cumin seeds
1 teaspoon turmeric
6 green cardamom pods, bruised lightly
2-3 whole cloves
4 garlic cloves, peeled and crushed
salt
2 potatoes, peeled and diced
1 large onion, peeled and finely sliced
25 g (1 oz) butter
1 teaspoon garam masala (page 16) or 1 teaspoon mild
    curry powder
600 ml (1 pint) coconut milk, using 225 g (8 oz) desiccated
    coconut and 750 ml (1¼ pints) boiling water (page 9)
juice of 1 lemon
few curry plant leaves or fresh coriander, to garnish
    (optional)
croûtes of fried bread sprinkled with mustard or poppy
    seeds, to serve

Preparation time: 35 minutes
Cooking time: 2½ hours

A favourite "old colonial" soup. This version is particularly enjoyable with the addition of the coconut
milk.

1. Place the beef and bones in a large pan with water.
Add the coriander, peppercorns, cumin, turmeric,
cardamom, cloves and garlic with salt to taste.
2. Bring to the boil and skim. Cover and simmer for
about 2 hours until the meat is tender. Cool slightly.
3. Lift out the bones and discard. Remove the meat,
shred finely and reserve. Strain the soup and remove
the spices.
4. Return 1.75 litres (3 pints) of the soup to the rinsed
pan with the potato. Bring to the boil, cover and cook
for 20 minutes until the potato is tender. Stir in the
reserved meat and set the pan aside.
5. In another large pan fry the onion in butter until just
beginning to colour. Add the garam masala or curry
powder. Remove from the heat and stir in the coconut
milk.
6. Stir the milk mixture into the soup. Add the lemon
juice and reheat without boiling to avoid curdling the
soup.
7. Serve in hot individual bowls with curry leaves or
coriander floating on top of each. Hand round croûtes
of fried bread sprinkled with the mustard or poppy
seeds.

HOME-MADE CURRY POWDERS

These quantities are a guide for the first time you make up your own curry powder. Thereafter you will decide on a little more of this and less of that till you strike the balance which suits your palate. Don't make large quantities, as once ground the flavours will deteriorate. However, if stored in a small plastic box in the freezer, the spices will keep for much longer without deterioration.

Hot:
2 teaspoons whole cloves
40 cardamom pods, bruised
large cinnamon stick
4 teaspoons cumin seeds
3 tablespoons coriander seeds
1 teaspoon fenugreek
1 teaspoon black peppercorns
1 tablespoon chilli powder or dried whole chillis
½ nutmeg, grated
1 tablespoon ground turmeric

Preparation time: 25 minutes
Cooking time: 10 minutes
Oven: 180°C, 350°F, Gas Mark 4

1. Place the cloves, cardamom and cinnamon stick on a baking sheet and bake in a preheated oven for 10 minutes.
2. In a heavy-based frying pan, dry fry the cumin, coriander, fenugreek and peppercorns. Stir constantly taking care not to burn the spices.
3. Break the cinnamon stick into pieces and remove the cardamom seeds from their pods. Grind all the spices together to a powder.
4. Transfer to an airtight container.

Mild:
2 tablespoons whole cloves
2 tablespoons black peppercorns
2 tablespoons cumin seeds
5 cm (2 inch) cinnamon stick
2 tablespoons cardamom pods, crushed lightly
3-4 bay leaves, dried
2 teaspoons nutmeg, grated (about ½ nutmeg)

Preparation time: 15 minutes
Cooking time: 5 minutes
Oven: 180°C, 350°F, Gas Mark 4

1. Place the cloves, peppercorns, cumin, cinnamon stick, cardamom pods and bay leaves on a baking sheet and bake in a preheated oven for 5 minutes, until the spices are giving off an aroma.

2. Break the cinnamon into pieces and remove the cardamom seeds from their pods. Grind all the spices together to a powder.
3. Add the freshly grated nutmeg and transfer to an airtight container.

Garam Masala:
4 tablespoons cumin seeds
2 tablespoons black peppercorns
24 cardamom pods, seeds removed
2 teaspoons whole cloves
large cinnamon stick

Preparation time: 15 minutes
Cooking time: 5 minutes
Oven: 180°C, 350°F, Gas Mark 4

1. Spread all the ingredients on a baking sheet and roast in the oven for 5 minutes, turning occasionally.
2. Break the cinnamon stick as finely as possible, then grind together with all the spices to produce a powder.
3. Store in an airtight container.

1. Chilli peppers   2. Dried chilli peppers   3. Ground chilli pepper
4. Paprika pepper   5. Black peppercorns   6. Cardomom pods   7. Cardomom seeds   8. Cinnamon quills   9. Fenugreek   10. Ground turmeric   11. Whole nutmegs   12. Cumin seeds   13. Coriander seeds   14. Whole cloves

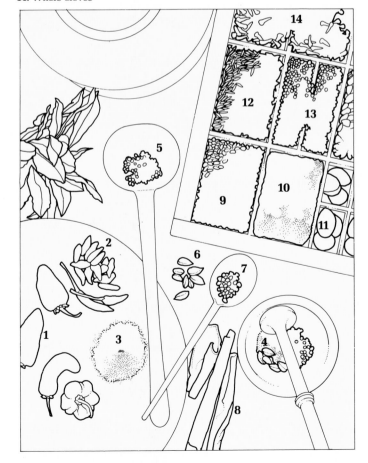

HOME STYLE TANDOORI CHICKEN

1.5 kg (3 lb) fresh chicken
juice of 1 lemon
1 teaspoon salt
8 green cardamom pods
2 teaspoons cumin seeds
1 teaspoon fennel seeds
2.5 cm (1 inch) piece of fresh ginger, scraped and chopped
   or 2 level teaspoons ground ginger
2-3 garlic cloves, peeled and crushed
1 teaspoon chilli powder
150 ml (¼ pint) plain unsweetened yogurt
25 g (1 oz) butter
coriander leaves, to garnish
naan or pitta bread, to serve

Preparation time: 30 minutes, plus marinating
Cooking time: about 1 hour
Oven: 220°C, 425°F, Gas Mark 7

The chicken may look overcooked because of the high cooking temperature but it will nevertheless taste juicy and delicious.

1. Wipe the chicken with paper towels. Remove the wing tips and cut the chicken in half lengthways through the backbone. Place skin side up in a large shallow ovenproof dish.
2. Using a small sharp knife, make several cuts into the chicken flesh, then rub in the lemon juice and salt.
3. Split open the cardamom pods and remove the small seeds. Place the cardamom, cumin and fennel seeds in a heavy-based frying pan. Cook without fat over a moderate heat for about 1-2 minutes, to bring out the flavour of the spices. Blend or grind to a powder and reserve.
4. Pound or blend the fresh ginger (if using) and garlic together. Add to the ground spices and ground ginger (if using) together with the chilli powder.
5. Mix all the spices with the yogurt and smother the chicken halves with the mixture. Stand for 5-6 hours to marinate.
6. Dot with butter and place in a preheated oven and cook for about 1 hour, basting twice in the first 30 minutes.
7. Cut each of the chicken halves through the centre, decorate with coriander leaves and serve immediately with naan or warmed pitta bread.

MILD CURRIED SCALLOPS

Serves 2-3
450 g (1 lb) frozen Queen scallops, thawed
1 garlic clove, peeled and crushed
1 small onion, peeled and chopped
about 4 tablespoons oil
2 teaspoons mild curry powder (page 16)
200 ml (⅓ pint) dry white wine
2 bay leaves
15 g (½ oz) butter
15 g (½ oz) flour
120 ml (4 fl oz) whipping or single cream
¼ teaspoon paprika pepper
curls of spring onion, to garnish (see below)

Preparation time: 15 minutes
Cooking time: 15 minutes

1. Dry the thawed scallops on paper towels and set aside.
2. Fry the garlic and onion in 3 tablespoons of the oil until softened without browning. Add the curry powder and fry, stirring constantly, to bring out the flavours.
3. Add the wine, bay leaves and scallops and bring to the boil. Cover and simmer gently for about 5 minutes, until the scallops are just tender. Lift out on to a serving dish and keep hot. Discard the bay leaves.
4. Make a beurre manié by creaming the butter and flour together to a paste. Return the sauce to the heat and add the butter and flour mixture in small pieces. Boil until thickened, stirring continuously.
5. Cool slightly, then pour some of the sauce into the cream contained in a bowl. Return the sauce and cream to the pan and reheat without boiling. Pour over the scallops.
6. Blend the paprika together with 2 teaspoons of the oil and pour over the surface of the dish in a pretty pattern.
7. Serve garnished with curls of spring onion and rice.

> Spring onion curls: this is a simple but effective vegetable garnish. Use spring onions that are a good colour and shape. Cut off the top green end from each spring onion, leaving a bulb end approximately 8 cm (3 inches) long. Using kitchen scissors or a small sharp knife, cut through the length of the spring onion bulb at regular intervals, without cutting right through the base of the onion. Plunge the cut spring onion bulb into a bowl of iced water and chill until the onions curl.

From the top right, clockwise: Mild curried scallops;
Home style Tandoori chicken; saffron; Lamb korma

LAMB KORMA

75 g (3 oz) unsalted butter
1 large onion, peeled and finely chopped
3 garlic cloves, peeled and crushed
2.5 cm (1 inch) piece of fresh ginger, scraped and cut into fine slivers
1 teaspoon chilli powder
1 tablespoon garam masala (page 16)
750 g (1½ lb) fillet end leg or shoulder of lamb, trimmed and cut into 2.5 cm (1 inch) cubes
150 ml (¼ pint) plain unsweetened yogurt
few strands of saffron soaked in 150 ml (¼ pint) warm water
salt
few stems of fresh coriander, to garnish

Preparation time: 25 minutes
Cooking time: 1 hour in heavy saucepan or 1¼ hours in oven
Oven: 160°C, 325°F, Gas Mark 3

Traditionally, a korma is a dry curry, but this one is moister and you might prefer it. As an alternative, eat with chapatis instead of rice.

1. Melt the butter in a pan and fry the onion, garlic and ginger, stirring frequently.
2. Mix the spices together, then add to the pan. Add the meat and seal the cubes on all sides tossing thoroughly in the spices.
3. Whisk the yogurt. Over a gentle heat gradually add the yogurt to the meat, stirring constantly to produce a smooth sauce.
4. Add the strained saffron water and salt. Stir well.
5. Cover and cook over a gentle heat until the meat is tender. Uncover for the final 15 minutes of the cooking time and add some extra water if the sauce reduces too much. Alternatively, cook in a covered casserole in a preheated oven.
6. Garnish with fresh coriander. Serve with wedges of lemon to squeeze over each helping and freshly boiled rice.

DHAL

175 g (6 oz) yellow split peas or lentils soaked in water
   overnight
450 ml (¾ pint) water
2 medium onions, peeled and finely chopped
2 garlic cloves, peeled and crushed
1 cm (½ inch) piece of fresh ginger, scraped and chopped
   or ½ teaspoon ground ginger
1 teaspoon ground turmeric
salt
2 tablespoons oil
2 teaspoons garam masala (page 16)
25 g (1 oz) butter, melted
fresh coriander leaves, to garnish

**Preparation time: 15 minutes, plus soaking overnight
and standing
Cooking time: 55 minutes**

This is a wonderful opportunity to use the home-made garam masala. The dhal is delicious served hot or warm, but do make sure that you allow time for it to stand, so that the full flavours emerge.

1. Drain the lentils, place in a medium saucepan and cover with the water. Add half the onion and garlic, all the ginger, turmeric powder and salt. Bring to the boil, cover and cook for 45 minutes or until tender and mushy.
2. Fry the remaining onion and garlic in the oil until just golden. Add the garam masala and cook for a further minute.
3. Stir the fried ingredients into the lentils. Do not cook further but leave for an hour or even longer, so that the flavours blend.
4. Taste and adjust the seasoning. Add the butter to the dhal and reheat until hot, stirring occasionally or reheat in a covered buttered dish in a preheated oven (190°C, 375°F, Gas Mark 5) for 25 minutes.
5. Serve sprinkled with fresh coriander leaves.

CHILLI CON CARNE

Serves 6
750 g (1½ lb) minced beef
6 tablespoons oil
2 medium onions, peeled and finely chopped
2 garlic cloves, peeled and crushed
1-2 teaspoons chilli powder
½ teaspoon cumin seeds
1 teaspoon chopped, fresh oregano, or ½ teaspoon dried oregano
3-4 tablespoons tomato purée
300 ml (½ pint) beef stock
salt
freshly ground black pepper
1 × 425 g (15 oz can) red kidney beans, drained
chopped fresh oregano or chives, to garnish

Preparation time: 30 minutes
Cooking time: 1 hour 15 minutes

In America chilli con carne is often served with a three bean salad, red and white kidney beans and chick peas, in a vinaigrette dressing and garnished with chopped spring onions. In this case omit the beans from the meat.

1. Lightly break up the meat with a fork and fry in half the oil until it begins to brown. Using a draining spoon transfer to a casserole.
2. Fry the onions and garlic in the remaining oil until just golden. Add the chilli powder (according to taste), cumin and oregano and cook over a gentle heat for a minute or two to bring out the flavours. Stir in the tomato purée.
3. Add this mixture to the meat in the casserole. Add the stock, salt and pepper to taste. Cover and cook gently for about 1 hour until the meat is tender.
4. Skim any fat from the surface of the casserole and stir in the red beans about 15 minutes before serving.
5. Serve in the casserole sprinkled with fresh oregano or chopped chives.

> If using dried red kidney beans, cover 175 g (6 oz) of the beans with cold water and leave to soak overnight. Drain, then rinse and drain again.
> To cook, place the beans in a large pan with plenty of cold water. Bring to the boil and ensure the beans are boiling properly for the first 10 minutes of cooking. Reduce the heat, cover and simmer for 1-1½ hours or until the beans are tender, adding a little salt towards the end of the cooking time.
> Drain the beans and use according to the recipe.

Chilli con carne

SURTEE CHICKEN CURRY

1 teaspoon salt
8 chicken pieces, about 1.5 kg (3 lb), skinned
2.5 cm (1 inch) piece of fresh ginger, scraped
2-3 garlic cloves, peeled and crushed
2-3 fresh green chillis
few sprigs fresh coriander
6 tablespoons oil
3 green cardamom pods, seeds removed
1 cinnamon stick
2-3 whole cloves
12 black peppercorns
2 medium onions, peeled and finely chopped
450 ml (¾ pint) water or chicken stock
Sauce:
300 ml (½ pint) milk
2 tablespoons desiccated coconut
1 tablespoon ground almonds
2 tablespoons cornflour
2 teaspoons poppy seeds, soaked in water for 15 minutes
To garnish:
4 hard-boiled eggs, shelled
a few fresh coriander leaves

Preparation time: 25 minutes
Cooking time: 50 minutes

1. Sprinkle the salt over the chicken pieces and set aside.
2. Pound or blend the ginger, garlic, chillis and leaves from the coriander until reduced to a paste.
3. Heat the oil in a deep frying pan and fry the cardamom seeds, cinnamon stick, cloves and peppercorns for 1 minute, stirring constantly.
4. Add the onions and fry until golden. Using a slotted draining spoon, lift out of the pan and reserve.
5. Add the chicken pieces to the pan and fry until sealed on all sides.
6. Stir the ginger, garlic, chilli and coriander mixture into the chicken and cook for 5 minutes. Add the stock or water, the reserved onions and more salt if necessary. Cover and simmer for about 40 minutes until the chicken is tender.
7. To prepare the sauce, place the milk, coconut and almonds in a pan. Bring to the boil. Blend a little cold water with the cornflour to make a paste, then stir into the milk and bring back to the boil, stirring constantly. Strain the poppy seeds through a fine sieve and add to the sauce.
8. Stir the sauce into the chicken curry and cook for just a few minutes.
9. Serve garnished with halves of hard-boiled egg and coriander leaves. Serve boiled rice as an accompaniment and a selection of side dishes such as mango chutney, sliced banana and rings of green pepper.

CHICKEN MARRAKESH

1.5 kg (3 lb) fresh chicken
6-7 tablespoons oil
1 garlic clove, peeled and crushed
2.5 cm (1 inch) piece of fresh ginger, scraped and cut into slivers
2 teaspoons ground turmeric
1 stick cinnamon
2-3 whole cloves
salt
freshly ground black pepper
900 ml (1½ pints) water
100 g (4 oz) ground almonds
To garnish:
wedges of lemon
fresh coriander leaves

Preparation time: 25 minutes
Cooking time: about 1 hour 10 minutes

An attractive supper party dish which goes well with a rice accompaniment.

1. Wipe the chicken with paper towels and truss if necessary.
2. Heat 4-5 tablespoons of the oil in a pan or flameproof casserole large enough to hold the chicken comfortably and fry the garlic, ginger, half the turmeric, the cinnamon and cloves for 2 minutes. Add the chicken and turn in the pan until well coloured with the turmeric.
3. Add the salt, pepper and water. Place the chicken, breast side down, in the casserole and bring to the boil. Cover and simmer for about 1 hour until the chicken is tender.
4. Strain off 450 ml (¾ pint) of the stock, skim off the fat and blend the stock with the ground almonds. Bring to the boil, stirring frequently, and cook, uncovered, for 2-3 minutes until the sauce thickens.
5. Transfer the chicken to a hot serving dish and remove the trussing strings. Pour over the almond sauce. Meanwhile blend the remaining turmeric powder and oil together, then drizzle over the chicken in the sauce.
6. Garnish the dish with wedges of lemon and fresh coriander leaves and serve with rice.

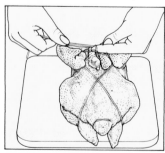
Trussing a chicken

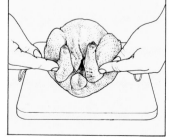
Knot string securely

SPICED PEACHES

1 kg (2¼ lb) peaches
1 orange, sliced
750 g (1½ lb) sugar
450 ml (¾ pint) light malt vinegar
12 whole cloves
24 allspice berries
1 cm (½ inch) piece of fresh ginger, scraped and bruised or 1 cm (½ inch) dried ginger root
5 cm (2 inch) cinnamon stick

Preparation time: 20 minutes
Cooking time: 25 minutes

Make several jars of these and give them away as welcome gifts around Christmas time.

1. Make a small incision around the stem area of the peaches. Place 4 at a time in a large pan of boiling water for 1-2 minutes. Lift out using a draining spoon and immediately transfer to a bowl of ice cold water to prevent further cooking. Repeat with the orange slices.
2. Carefully remove the skins from the peaches and set aside.
3. Place the sugar and vinegar in a large pan and stir over a medium heat until the sugar has dissolved.
4. Place the cloves, allspice, ginger (fresh or dried) and cinnamon stick into a muslin bag. Tie up and drop into the pan.
5. Lower the peaches into this syrup and simmer gently for about 8 minutes, until just tender. Take care not to overcook. Transfer the peaches to a large glass jar or suitable container.
6. Cook the orange slices in the syrup for 3-4 minutes and arrange in the jar with the peaches. Remove the spice bag and boil the syrup for 3-4 minutes to concentrate the flavour.
7. Pour over the peaches, cool, then cover and seal. Leave in a cool place for at least a month. Serve with roast pork or goose or a ham.

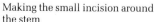
Making the small incision around the stem

After blanching, plunge into ice-cold water

From the top: Piri piri prawns; Piri piri queen scallops

PIRI PIRI PRAWNS

675 g (1½ lb) large fresh or frozen prawns
¾-1 teaspoon chilli powder
½-1 teaspoon salt
juice of 1 lemon
oil, for deep frying
To garnish:
wedges of lemon
fresh coriander leaves

Preparation time: 15 minutes, plus marinating
Cooking time: 1-2 minutes

This recipe comes from Mozambique. The prawns are expensive but are luxurious for a special occasion.

1. Thaw the prawns if frozen. Remove the heads and body shell from the prawns but leave on the tails. If preferred, make a small incision down the spine of the prawn to remove the black spinal cord.
2. Combine the chilli powder, salt and lemon juice and marinate the prawns in the mixture for about 1 hour.
3. Deep fry in oil heated to 185°C, 360°F (or until a cube of bread browns in 3 seconds) for 1-2 minutes. Do not overcook.
4. Serve very hot, garnished with lemon wedges and coriander leaves. Have finger bowls on the table or paper napkins at the ready, if the prawns are served at a cocktail party.

Variation:
Use 675 g (1½ lb) Queen scallops as a substitute for the prawns. Thaw completely and dry on paper towels before putting in the marinade. Deep fry, allowing an extra minute or two if necessary.

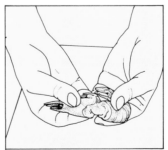

1 Remove heads from prawns
2 Carefully take off the body shells and remove any spawn
3 Make a fine incision in the back of each prawn and remove spinal cord

BOBOTIE

Serves 6

2 medium onions, peeled and finely chopped
5 tablespoons oil
750 g (1½ lb) minced beef
1 tablespoon mild curry powder (page 16)
1 teaspoon ground turmeric
2 tablespoons wine vinegar
2 tomatoes, peeled and chopped
150 ml (¼ pint) beef stock
salt
1 large slice white or brown bread, soaked in milk
25 g (1 oz) chopped almonds
75 g (3 oz) sultanas
1 tablespoon brown sugar
1 tablespoon apricot jam or mango chutney
2 eggs
300 ml (½ pint) milk
thin slices of lemon
3-4 fresh bay leaves

Preparation time: 30 minutes
Cooking time: 1 hour 20 minutes
Oven: 180°C, 350°F, Gas Mark 4

Bobotie is a traditional South African dish and is to that part of the world what moussaka is to the Greeks. It's an attractive party dish.

1. Fry the onions in the oil until golden. Add the meat and stir until just beginning to brown.
2. Blend the curry powder and turmeric with the vinegar and stir into the meat. Add the stock, tomatoes and salt and cook uncovered for 15 minutes.
3. Squeeze the milk from the bread. Break the bread into small pieces, then stir into the meat mixture together with the almonds, sultanas, brown sugar, jam or chutney.
4. Spoon into a shallow, buttered casserole. Bake in a preheated oven for 30 minutes.
5. Beat the eggs with the milk and add a little salt. Strain over the meat. Arrange lemon slices and bay leaves in the custard. Return to the oven for a further 30 minutes until the custard is set.
6. Serve with rice and salad.

Variation:
Try minced lamb instead of the beef, which is also delicious.

LAMBS' LIVER ALBANIAN STYLE

1 medium onion, peeled and thinly sliced and sprinkled
  with salt
½ teaspoon cayenne pepper
3 tablespoons finely chopped Continental or English
  parsley
450 g (1 lb) fresh lambs' or calves' liver, cut into finger size
  strips
4 tablespoons Pernod or Ouzo
2 tablespoons seasoned flour (page 26)
6 tablespoons olive oil
1 red pepper, deseeded and cut into rings or strips

Preparation time: 20 minutes, plus marinating
Cooking time: 2-3 minutes

1. Allow the onion and salt to rest for 30 minutes then
rinse, drain and dry thoroughly. Combine with the
cayenne and parsley.
2. Marinate the liver strips in Pernod or Ouzo for 15
minutes, then drain and dry on paper towels.
3. Toss the liver in seasoned flour and fry in hot oil for
2-3 minutes only, until just beginning to brown.
Quickly drain on paper towels.
5. Pile the liver on to a hot serving dish. Garnish with
the onion mixture and the red pepper rings or strips.
6. Serve with freshly boiled Basmatti rice.

GROUNDNUT STEW

Serves 4-6
1 large onion, peeled and chopped
6 tablespoons oil
1.5 kg (3 lb) fresh chicken, jointed into 8 pieces
225 g (8 oz) roasted peanuts, ground to a paste or 175 g
  (6 oz) peanut butter
450 ml (¾ pint) chicken stock
3 large tomatoes, peeled and chopped
1-2 teaspoons chilli powder
¼-½ teaspoon ground cumin
salt
To garnish:
4-6 hard-boiled eggs
paprika pepper, for dusting

Preparation time: 25 minutes
Cooking time: 1¼-1½ hours
Oven: 180°C, 350°F, Gas Mark 4

A West African chicken stew, marvellous for a simple
supper party or a Sunday lunch. The sauce can also be
made separately to pour over any left-over chicken or
even turkey on Boxing Day. As an alternative, use com-
mercially prepared peanut butter to cut the corners in
preparation.

1. In a deep frying pan, fry the onion in oil until golden brown. Fry the chicken joints to seal in the juices.
Lift out, drain and keep to one side.
2. Remove the pan from the heat and stir in the ground
peanuts or peanut butter and stock to produce a sauce
resembling thin cream.
3. Add the tomatoes, ground chilli powder, cumin,
salt and chicken joints. Cover and simmer for 1¼-1½
hours until the chicken is tender. Alternatively, cook
in a preheated oven for the same time.
4. Add the shelled hard-boiled eggs about 5 minutes
before serving.
5. Transfer to a hot serving dish and dust with
paprika.
6. Serve with plain boiled rice, mango chutney, sliced
banana and sliced green pepper.

From the left: Bobotie; Lambs' liver Albanian style; Groundnut stew

STIFADO

Serves 6

1 kg (2 lb) lean chuck or shin of beef, trimmed and cut into
    2.5 cm (1 inch) cubes
50 g (2 oz) seasoned flour (see below)
5 tablespoons oil
½ teaspoon cumin seeds
5 cm (2 inch) piece cinnamon stick
3 tablespoons tomato purée
3 tablespoons herb vinegar
900 ml (1½ pints) beef stock
salt
freshly ground black pepper
few sprigs of fresh thyme
450 g (1 lb) small onions, peeled
100 g (4 oz) feta cheese, cut into cubes
thyme or parsley, to garnish

Preparation time: 30 minutes
Cooking time: 2¾ hours
Oven: 160°C, 325°F, Gas Mark 3

The combination of spices, herbs and feta cheese gives
this casserole a very special flavour. Try it for a Sunday
lunch served with jacket baked potatoes sprinkled
with plenty of salt before baking.

1. Using a large polythene bag, toss the meat in the
seasoned flour.
2. Fry in the heated oil, turning constantly, until the
meat begins to brown. Transfer to a covered casserole.
3. Add the cumin, cinnamon stick and tomato purée
to the remaining juices. Stir in the vinegar, stock, salt
and pepper to taste and thyme. Bring to the boil.
4. Pour over the meat, cover and cook in a preheated
oven for about 2 hours until the meat is almost tender.
5. Plunge the onions into boiling water, drain and add
to the casserole. Cook for a further 30 minutes.
6. Add the cubes of cheese and return uncovered to
the oven for a few minutes, until the cheese begins to
melt. Serve from the casserole scattered liberally with
thyme or parsley.

Variation:
Rabbit can also be used in this traditional Greek recipe
– you would need 2 medium size rabbits prepared and
jointed by the butcher.

Seasoned flour:
To each 50 g (2 oz) plain flour or cornflour add ½
teaspoon salt and a little freshly ground black pepper.

From the left: Stifado; Goulash soup

DEVILLED KIDNEYS

8 fresh lambs' kidneys, skinned, halved and cored
25 g (1 oz) butter
1 small onion, peeled and finely chopped
2 teaspoons hot curry powder (page 16)
1 tablespoon Worcestershire sauce
2 tablespoons redcurrant jelly or mango chutney
150 ml (¼ pint) stock or water
salt
freshly ground black pepper
150 ml (¼ pint) double cream
squeeze of lemon juice
chopped parsley, to garnish

Preparation time: 20 minutes
Cooking time: 20 minutes

GOULASH SOUP

2 tablespoons oil
2 onions, peeled and finely chopped
1 garlic clove, peeled and crushed
350 g (12 oz) piece shin of beef, trimmed and diced into
   0.5 cm (¼ inch) cubes
1 tablespoon paprika pepper
1 tablespoon caraway seeds
1 tablespoon tomato purée
1.25 litres (2¼ pints) beef stock
salt
freshly ground black pepper
1 large potato, peeled and finely diced
1 carrot, peeled and finely diced
1 tablespoon chopped fresh parsley
150 ml (¼ pint) plain unsweetened yogurt or soured cream,
   to serve

Preparation time: 25 minutes
Cooking time: 1 hour 20 minutes

A good wholesome soup. Ideal for a chilly night or lunch at the weekend.

1. Heat the oil in a large pan and fry the onion and garlic without browning.
2. Increase the heat, stir in the meat and brown on all sides. Reduce the heat and add the paprika and caraway seeds.
3. Stir in the tomato purée and slowly add the stock. Add salt and pepper to taste.
4. Cover and cook for about 1 hour, until the meat is tender.
5. Add the potato and carrots and return to the boil. Simmer, cover and cook for a further 20 minutes, until the vegetables are just tender. Stir in the parsley. Taste and adjust the seasoning.
6. Serve in hot bowls and top each helping with a spoonful of soured cream or yogurt. Try this soup with the Onion and parsley party loaf (page 38).

Paprika pepper gives Goulash its distinctive and authentic flavour. It is also renowned for flavouring the dish Paprika Chicken. Try a little paprika added to sauces to pour over poached chicken breasts or fish, or as a delicate garnish for egg, cheese and fish dishes.

Caraway seeds are also an important ingredient in Goulash. The Germans and Austrians are passionate about them, using them in cakes, bread, sauerkraut, cheese dishes and sprinkled over roast pork. Try adding them to potato or beetroot salad, and to cooked red cabbage.

1. Rinse and dry the kidneys on paper towels.
2. Heat the butter in a frying pan and fry the kidneys on both sides for 3 minutes. Drain, then transfer to a dish and keep warm.
3. Fry the onion in the juices remaining in the pan. Stir in the curry powder, Worcestershire sauce and redcurrant jelly or chutney and cook for a minute or two. Then pour in the stock, season with salt and pepper and cook for 10 minutes.
4. Pour a ladleful of sauce into a bowl and stir in the cream. Away from the heat, pour this mixture back into the pan.
5. Return the kidneys to the sauce and reheat gently without allowing the sauce to boil. Sharpen the flavour with lemon juice if liked.
6. Transfer to a hot serving dish. Sprinkle with parsley and serve with freshly boiled rice.

Variation:
450 g (1 lb) chicken livers can be used instead of the lambs' kidneys. If frozen, allow at least 12 hours to thaw before using.

SUBTLE FLAVOURS

STUFFED VINE LEAVES

Serves 6-8

1 × 225 g (8 oz) packet vine leaves *or* 300 g (11 oz) canned
   or bottled vine leaves, drained
100 g (4 oz) long-grain rice
225 g (8 oz) lamb or beef, minced
1 large tomato, skinned and chopped
1 small onion, peeled and chopped
2 tablespoons chopped fresh mint
2 tablespoons chopped fresh parsley
50 g (2 oz) pine kernels, chopped
3 tablespoons tomato purée (optional)
salt
freshly ground black pepper
½ teaspoon ground cinnamon
450 ml (¾ pint) water
juice of a large lemon

Preparation time: 20 minutes, plus soaking
Cooking time: 30-40 minutes

Vine leaves are usually preserved in a brine solution and must be soaked thoroughly before using. Pour boiling water over them in a large bowl. Stand for 20 minutes, then drain and rinse with cold water. Repeat the process. Handle with care, as the leaves are very fragile.

1. Place the prepared vine leaves on paper towels to drain.
2. Pour boiling water over the rice and leave to stand whilst preparing the rest of the filling.
3. Fork through the beef or lamb in a bowl, add the tomato, onion, herbs, pine kernels, tomato purée (if using), salt, pepper and cinnamon. Drain the rice thoroughly and add to the mixture.
4. Use any torn leaves to line the base of a flameproof casserole. Place a vine leaf on a board with the stem facing. Place a small spoonful of the filling on to the leaf, roll into a sausage shape, tucking in at the side pieces whilst rolling. Repeat with the remaining leaves and mixture. Lay side by side in the casserole and set a plate on top to keep the rolls firm.
5. Pour 150 ml (¼ pint) of the water and the lemon juice over the rolls. Replace the plate and bring to the boil, reduce to a gentle simmer and cook for 30-40 minutes until the filling is tender, adding more water if necessary.
6. Serve hot with fresh bread for lunch or supper.

FENNEL SOUP

500 g (1¼ lb) fish trimmings, washed and drained
1.5 litres (2½ pints) water
1 onion, peeled and sliced
1 carrot, peeled and sliced
1 celery stick, washed and sliced
few sprigs of parsley
450 g (1 lb) fennel bulbs, washed
bay leaf
salt
freshly ground black pepper
2 lemons
3 egg yolks
1 teaspoon Pernod (optional)

Preparation time: 25 minutes
Cooking time: 45 minutes

1. Place the fish trimmings in a large pan and cover with cold water. Add the onion, carrot, celery and sprigs of parsley.
2. Cut the feathery leaves from the top of the fennel and reserve for garnish. Cut the fennel bulb into quarters and place in the pan with the bay leaf, salt and pepper.
3. Bring to the boil, skim if necessary, then cover and cook for 35-40 minutes until the vegetables are tender.
4. Strain the stock from the vegetables and fish into a clean pan. Reduce the liquid by boiling to about 1 litre (1¾ pints).
5. Cut 4 slices from the lemons and reserve for garnish. Squeeze the juice from the remainder and add to the egg yolks. Whisk well, then pour in 150 ml (¼ pint) of the hot, not boiling, stock.
6. Return this to the pan and place over a gentle heat, stirring constantly without allowing to boil.
7. Taste and adjust the seasoning and add a little Pernod, if liked.
8. Serve in hot bowls with a slice of lemon and feathery fennel leaves floating on top.

From the top, left: sprigs of fennel; fresh bay leaves;
Fennel soup; fennel bulbs; mint; Stuffed vine leaves; parsley

BAKED HAM WITH SPICED PEACHES

1 joint of bacon, about 1.75 kg (4 lb) (if smoked, soak
   overnight in cold water)
½ teaspoon allspice berries
4 bay leaves
2.5 cm (1 inch) piece of fresh ginger, scraped and finely
   shredded
Glaze:
1 tablespoon French mustard
2 tablespoons syrup from spiced peaches
50 g (2 oz) demerara sugar
slices of fresh orange, to garnish
spiced peaches (page 22), to serve

Preparation time: 10 minutes, plus soaking
Cooking time: about 2 hours 10 minutes
Oven: 220°C, 425°F, Gas Mark 7

This is a simple and foolproof way of cooking a ham
no matter what size the joint may be. The quantity of
glaze may need to be increased for a larger ham.

1. Drain then weigh the meat and calculate the cooking time allowing 25 minutes per 450 g (1 lb).
2. Wrap completely in a foil parcel with the allspice, bay leaves and shredded ginger sprinkled all over the meat.
3. Place the parcel in a roasting tin and cook in a preheated oven for the calculated time, *less* half an hour.
4. Remove from the oven, allow to stand for 15 minutes. Open the foil and remove the allspice and bay leaves. Strip off the rind which will come away easily, and using a sharp knife score the fat.
5. For the glaze, blend the mustard, peach syrup and sugar together and cover the scored fat with this mixture.
6. Return the meat to the oven for a further 30 minutes without covering, basting occasionally, until the outside is golden.
7. Before carving, allow the ham to stand in a warm place for 15 minutes covered loosely with the foil. It will then be easier to carve.
8. Arrange on a serving platter, garnished with orange slices and a bowl of spiced peaches to serve.

SOUTHERN FRIED CHICKEN

4 fresh chicken quarters, about 1.5 kg (3 lb) chicken, quartered
50 g (2 oz) tarragon butter (page 38)
50 g (2 oz) maître d'hôtel butter (page 38)
40 g (1½ oz) seasoned flour (page 26)
50 g (2 oz) butter
150 ml (¼ pint) single cream
salt
freshly ground black pepper
To garnish:
chopped fresh parsley
chopped fresh tarragon

Preparation time: 15 minutes, plus resting
Cooking time: 35-40 minutes

Try spreading herb butters on fish and grilled or fried meats before cooking.

1. Wipe the chicken, then spread the skin with a mixture of the tarragon and maître d'hôtel butters. Chill for about 1 hour until the butter is firm.
2. Gently toss each quarter in a polythene bag containing the seasoned flour until well coated. Fry in the butter until brown on both sides.
3. Stir in the cream, salt and pepper. Cover with a lid or a piece of foil and continue to cook for about 25-35 minutes until the chicken is tender.
4. Serve garnished with parsley and tarragon, accompanied with bread, or rice and a salad.

SESAME CHICKEN

1 fresh chicken 1.25 kg (2½ lb), jointed into 4 or 4 chicken quarters
50 g (2 oz) sesame seeds, dry-fried in a heavy based frying pan for 2 minutes
50 ml (2 fl oz) oil
1 medium onion, peeled and finely chopped
1 garlic clove, peeled and crushed
2.5 cm (1 inch) piece of fresh ginger, scraped and pounded
½ teaspoon chilli powder or cayenne pepper
25 g (1 oz) fresh breadcrumbs

Preparation time: 20 minutes
Cooking time: 1 hour
Oven: 190°C, 375°F, Gas Mark 5

Mix sesame seeds with seasoned flour or in a light egg and crumb coating for fried chicken or fish.

1. Wipe and place the chicken quarters skin side down in a lightly oiled shallow roasting tin.
2. Mix half the fried sesame seeds with the oil, onion, garlic, ginger and chilli powder or cayenne. Mix well, then spoon evenly over the chicken pieces.
3. Roast in a preheated oven for 30 minutes, then turn the chicken pieces over. Baste with the juices in the pan.
4. Mix the remaining sesame seeds with the breadcrumbs and scatter over the chicken joints. Bake for a further 30 minutes or until tender and golden.
5. Serve the chicken with a bowl of plain unsweetened yogurt, tomato and cucumber salad and bread.

From the left: Baked ham with Spiced peaches; savoury butters; tarragon; Southern fried chicken

LAMB PERSILLÉ

Serves 6

2 whole loins of lamb or best end of neck (6 chops each), skinned and chined
50 g (2 oz) mint butter (page 38)
salt
freshly ground black pepper

Herb mixture:

75 g (3 oz) fresh breadcrumbs
2 teaspoons chopped fresh parsley
2 teaspoons chopped fresh mint
2 teaspoons chopped fresh coriander or ½ teaspoon crushed coriander seeds
grated rind of ½ lemon
50-75 g (2-3 oz) butter, melted
fresh watercress, to garnish

Preparation time: 20 minutes
Cooking time: 1 hour 20 minutes
Oven: 180°C, 350°F, Gas Mark 4;
      200°C, 400°F, Gas Mark 6

1. Wipe the meat, then spread the mint butter on to the fat. Season with salt and pepper and place in a roasting tin. Roast in a preheated oven for about 1 hour, basting once or twice.

2. Meanwhile prepare the herb mixture. Place the breadcrumbs, herbs, lemon rind, salt and pepper in a bowl. Bind loosely with the melted butter.

3. Remove the lamb joints from the oven and increase the oven temperature.

4. Press the herb mixture on to the fat of the meat and return to the oven to brown for 20 minutes.

5. Garnish with watercress. To serve, cut down between the chined bone with a sharp knife, so that everyone gets cutlets with a crisp coating.

PORK CHOPS WITH GREEN PEPPERCORNS IN CREAM SAUCE

4 thick pork chops, about 225 g (8 oz) each
50 g (2 oz) butter
2 tablespoons oil
salt
150 ml (¼ pint) double cream
2 teaspoons lemon juice
1½ tablespoons drained green peppercorns
100 g (4 oz) button mushrooms, wiped
chopped fresh parsley, to garnish

Preparation time: 20 minutes
Cooking time: 1¼ hours
Oven: 180°C, 350°F, Gas Mark 4

Peppercorns grow on a vine – the fruit being picked when its colour changes from green to red and yellow. Green peppercorns come in small cans preserved in brine and are available in delicatessens, Eastern food specialists and some supermarkets. Black peppercorns are ripened in the sun. White peppercorns are the same ripe peppercorns soaked in running water for a week, then rubbed to remove the outer skin.

White pepper is not as powerful and aromatic as black pepper.

1. Wipe the chops, then fry in half the butter and oil for 5 minutes on each side to brown. Transfer into a large shallow casserole and sprinkle with the salt.
2. Drain the excess fat from the pan, retaining the juices. Stir in the cream and lemon juice and allow to come to the boil. Add the peppercorns, then pour evenly over the chops.
3. Cover with foil and cook in a preheated oven for 1 hour. Remove the foil and cook for a further 10 minutes.
4. Serve from the casserole surrounded by button mushrooms fried in the remaining butter and sprinkle with chopped parsley. Serve rice separately.

Variation:
Use veal or bacon chops in place of the pork. Reduce the cooking time according to size. Use less salt with bacon chops.

TIAN

450 g (1 lb) young courgettes, trimmed and cut into 2.5 cm (1 inch) chunks
salt
50 g (2 oz) butter
1 small onion, peeled and chopped
1 garlic clove, peeled and crushed
225 g (8 oz) tomatoes, skinned and chopped
1 teaspoon sugar
1 × 400 g (14 oz) can tomatoes, chopped
2 tablespoons chopped fresh herbs, e.g. parsley, chives, and basil
4 eggs, beaten
50 g (2 oz) Parmesan cheese, finely grated
freshly ground black pepper

Preparation time: 25 minutes
Cooking time: 25-30 minutes
Oven: 190°C, 375°F, Gas Mark 5

A Tian is a shallow earthenware dish usually 23 cm (9 inches) in diameter. This recipe is particularly versatile and can be served hot for lunch or supper, or taken on a picnic and cut into wedges like a cake. A little diced cooked potato or cooked rice can be added to the mixture, but do not add too much or the tian might become too firm.

1. Brush the tian with oil and line with a circle of non-stick silicone paper. This is especially advisable if the tian is to be turned out and served cold.
2. Place the courgettes sprinkled with a teaspoon of salt in a saucepan and heat gently until the juices begin to run. Add half the butter, cover and cook gently for 5-8 minutes or until just tender. Do not overcook. Using a slotted draining spoon, transfer the courgettes into a bowl and reserve.
3. Melt the remaining butter and fry the onion and garlic until soft but not brown. Add the tomatoes, salt and sugar and cook for 5 minutes. Add the canned tomatoes and half the herbs. Cook uncovered for a further 10-15 minutes until most of the liquid has evaporated and the tomato mixture has thickened.
4. Add the tomato mixture to the courgettes. Cool slightly, then mix in the beaten eggs, Parmesan cheese, remaining herbs, salt and pepper.
5. Turn into the prepared tian dish and bake in a preheated oven for 20-25 minutes, until well risen and firm to the touch. Serve hot or cold with green salad and bread.

From the top left: mint; coriander; chives; Lamb persillé; Tian

AUBERGINE BAKE

Serves 8
750 g (1¾ lb) aubergines
Tomato sauce:
1 small onion, peeled and finely chopped
2 garlic cloves, peeled and crushed
1 tablespoon oil
15 g (½ oz) butter
750 g (1½ lb) ripe tomatoes, peeled and roughly chopped
salt
freshly ground black pepper
1 teaspoon sugar
2 tablespoons chopped fresh herbs, parsley, basil, marjoram
1-2 tablespoons tomato purée (optional)
Topping:
50-75 g (2-3 oz) fresh white or brown breadcrumbs
2 tablespoons chopped fresh parsley
2 tablespoons chopped fresh basil
a little oil

Preparation time: 50 minutes
Cooking time: 1 hour
Oven: 150°C, 300°F, Gas Mark 2;
       180°C, 350°F, Gas Mark 4

Blanching aubergines results in a less oily dish which most people prefer. This dish can be served hot, warm or cold. Try it warm with yogurt for lunch or hot with roast lamb.

1. Cut the aubergines into 1 cm (½ inch) slices. Plunge half into a large pan of boiling water and cook for 3 minutes. Drain in a colander lined with paper towels. Then repeat with the remaining aubergines.
2. To make the tomato sauce, fry the onion and garlic in hot oil and butter until soft and transparent. Add the tomatoes, salt, pepper, sugar and herbs. Simmer uncovered over a medium heat until the tomatoes are soft and the sauce is beginning to thicken. Tomato purée can be added to improve the colour.
3. Cover the base of an oiled shallow ovenproof dish with half the aubergine slices. Cover with half the prepared tomato sauce. Sprinkle with half the breadcrumbs, herbs and drizzle a little oil over the top. Add salt and pepper.
4. Repeat the layers with the remaining ingredients and bake in the preheated oven for about 45 minutes, then increase the oven temperature and cook for a further 15 minutes.

STUFFED SHOULDER OF LAMB TURKISH STYLE

1 shoulder of lamb 1.5 kg (3½ lb), boned
salt
freshly ground black pepper
Stuffing:
1 small onion, peeled and finely chopped
15 g (½ oz) butter
25 g (1 oz) pine kernels
25 g (1 oz) rice
50 ml (2 fl oz) water
1 teaspoon coriander seeds, crushed
a little grated nutmeg
grated rind and juice of 1 orange
25 g (1 oz) raisins
fresh coriander leaves, to garnish

Preparation time: 40 minutes
Cooking time: about 1¾ hours
Oven: 180°C, 350°F, Gas Mark 4

1. Wipe the shoulder of lamb. Sprinkle with salt and pepper and set aside.
2. To make the stuffing, fry the onion in the butter until soft and transparent. Add the pine kernels and rice. Stir well, then add water and a little salt. Bring to the boil, then reduce the heat. Cover and cook gently for 8 minutes until the rice is almost tender.
3. Remove from the heat and stir in the coriander, nutmeg, half the orange rind and the raisins. Cool. Use the mixture to fill the cavity of the shoulder of lamb. Sew up the cavity using a trussing needle and fine string to form the shoulder into a neat shape. Do not sew up tightly.
4. Sprinkle the outside of the shoulder with more salt and pepper and roast in a preheated oven for 1¾-2 hours.
5. Strain the fat from the meat juices, then pour the juices into a small pan. Add the remaining orange rind and all the orange juice. Taste and adjust the seasoning and reheat.
6. Carve the lamb into thick slices and serve on a hot platter garnished with lots of fresh coriander, accompanied by the sauce.

From the left: Aubergine bake;
Stuffed shoulder of lamb – Turkish style

ROAST CHICKEN WITH TARRAGON

1 fresh chicken, 1.5 kg (3 lb)
50 g (2 oz) tarragon butter, softened (page 38)
salt
freshly ground black pepper
1 lemon, halved
few sprigs of fresh tarragon, to garnish

Preparation time: 10 minutes
Cooking time: 1 hour
Oven: 190°C, 375°F, Gas Mark 5

1. Wipe the chicken, then place one hand under the skin at the neck end to ease the skin away from the breast and thigh meat.
2. Spread half the tarragon butter under the skin, and the remaining half in the body cavity. Replace the neck flap and secure with fine string or a small skewer.
3. Sprinkle the chicken with salt and pepper. Roast in a preheated oven for 50 minutes, basting once or twice during cooking.
4. Squeeze the juice from one half of the lemon over the chicken breast and return to the oven for a further 10 minutes.
5. Serve, garnished with sprigs of fresh tarragon and the remaining lemon cut into wedges.

VEAL GOULASH WITH HERB DUMPLINGS

Serves 6

1 kg (2 lb) pie veal, cut into 2.5 cm (1 inch) cubes
3 tablespoons seasoned flour (page 26)
4-5 tablespoons oil
450 g (1 lb) onions, peeled and finely chopped
1 garlic clove, peeled and crushed
2 tablespoons paprika pepper
1 tablespoon tomato purée
600 ml (1 pint) tomato juice or water and stock cube
1 teaspoon caraway seeds
Herb dumplings:
75 g (3 oz) fresh white breadcrumbs
75 g (3 oz) shredded suet
75 g (3 oz) self-raising flour
2-3 tablespoons chopped fresh mixed herbs, tarragon,
    parsley, thyme and marjoram
salt
freshly ground black pepper
2 eggs, beaten
150 ml (¼ pint) soured cream or double cream with
    2 teaspoons lemon juice
To garnish:
¼ of a green pepper, cored, seeded and cut into strips
¼ of a red pepper, cored, seeded and cut into strips

Preparation time: 40 minutes
Cooking time: 1¾-2 hours
Oven: 160°C, 325°F, Gas Mark 3

1. Toss the meat in the seasoned flour, then fry in hot oil until browned on all sides. Using a slotted draining spoon, transfer to a flameproof casserole.
2. Fry the onions and garlic in the remaining oil until they begin to soften. Stir in the paprika, tomato purée, tomato juice or water and stock cube and caraway seeds. Pour over the meat then cover and cook in a preheated oven for 1½-1¾ hours or until the meat is tender.
3. Meanwhile prepare the dumplings. Mix together the breadcrumbs, suet, flour, herbs and seasoning. Bind to a soft dough with beaten egg. Divide the mixture into 18 equal portions and roll into ball shapes.
4. Fifteen minutes before serving, remove the casserole from the oven. Taste and adjust the seasoning. Place the casserole over a high heat and bring to the boil, then drop in the dumplings. Reduce to a simmer, then cover and cook until the dumplings are light and fluffy.
5. To serve, arrange the dumplings round the edge of a heated serving dish. Stir the soured cream into the goulash. Reheat, without boiling, stirring constantly, then ladle into the centre of the dish. Garnish with the strips of red and green pepper. Serve with baked jacket potatoes and a seasonal green vegetable.

FRIKADELLER

450 g (1 lb) lean veal, finely minced
1 small onion, peeled and finely chopped
25 g (1 oz) fresh breadcrumbs
1 tablespoon chopped fresh parsley
salt
freshly ground black pepper
a little grated nutmeg
1 egg, beaten
seasoned flour (page 26)
oil, for frying
Lemon and tarragon sauce:
75 g (3 oz) butter
1 garlic clove, peeled and crushed
1½ tablespoons flour
200 ml (⅓ pint) chicken stock
1-2 tablespoons sugar
grated rind and juice of a large lemon
1 tablespoon chopped fresh tarragon
dash of Tabasco sauce

Preparation time: 20 minutes
Cooking time: 12 minutes

These little meat balls can be served either with the lemon and tarragon sauce below, or with a hot chilli tomato ketchup at a drinks party. They are popular as a children's supper with a home-made tomato sauce (see Aubergine Bake, page 34) and noodles. Do not let the tomato sauce thicken up so much for this recipe.

1. Mix the veal with the onion, breadcrumbs, parsley, salt, pepper and nutmeg. Bind with as much egg as necessary to make a soft but non-sticky mixture.
2. With wet hands roll the mixture into about 24 small balls the size of a walnut and toss in the seasoned flour.
3. Fry in hot oil for 8 minutes until browned all over and keep warm.
4. To make the sauce, melt the butter in a pan and then fry the garlic without browning. Add the flour and cook gently for a few seconds, stirring constantly.
5. Away from the heat, stir in the stock. When thoroughly blended, return to the heat, stirring until the sauce begins to thicken.
6. Add the sugar, lemon rind and juice, herbs and Tabasco. Serve hot with the meat balls.

Variation:
Use minced beef in place of veal and serve with tomato sauce (page 34).

From the left, clockwise: Frikadeller; Danish hot potato salad;
Veal goulash with herb dumplings; fresh herbs from the top:
marjoram; thyme; tarragon; parsley; chives

DANISH HOT POTATO SALAD

750 g (1½ lb) potatoes, washed
6 rashers streaky bacon, rind removed
1 small onion, peeled and finely chopped
120 ml (4 fl oz) tarragon or herb vinegar
120 ml (4 fl oz) water
2 tablespoons caster sugar
1 teaspoon salt
freshly ground black pepper
1 small green pepper, cored, seeded and cut into strips
2 eggs, hard-boiled, sliced or chopped
2 tablespoons chopped fresh chives or parsley

Preparation time: 20 minutes
Cooking time: about 30 minutes

To make herb vinegar, pour 600 ml (1 pint) warmed wine vinegar into a wide-necked jar containing 300 ml (½ pint) of fresh herbs. Cover and leave for 3-4 weeks. Stir daily, strain and use.

1. Place the potatoes in a pan of water and cook until just tender. Remove the skins, then slice or dice and keep hot.
2. Fry or grill the bacon until crisp. Reserve the fat. Drain on paper towels, then crumble and set aside.
3. Fry the onion in the bacon fat until soft and transparent. Add the vinegar, water, sugar, salt and pepper. Allow to boil for 1-2 minutes to concentrate the flavour, then pour over the hot potatoes and toss together.
4. Turn out on to a hot serving dish, sprinkle the green pepper, reserved bacon, egg and chives over the top.

ONION AND PARSLEY PARTY LOAF

Serves 8
225 g (8 oz) plain strong flour
225 g (8 oz) wholemeal flour
2 teaspoons salt
2 teaspoons sugar
50 g (2 oz) butter
150 ml (¼ pint) water, at blood heat
2 teaspoons dried yeast
150 ml (¼ pint) milk, warmed
Filling:
1 large onion, peeled and finely chopped
2 tablespoons chopped fresh parsley

Preparation time: 10 minutes, plus rising
Cooking time: 35-40 minutes
Oven: 230°C, 450°F, Gas Mark 8;
200°C, 400°F, Gas Mark 6

This is a perfect party loaf as each person can pull off a portion easily. It teams well with soups for a family lunch or supper.

1. Sift flours and salt into a bowl with 1 teaspoon of the sugar and rub in 15 g (½ oz) of the butter.
2. Dissolve the remaining sugar in the warm water, sprinkle in the yeast and stand for 10-15 minutes, until frothy. Add to the dry ingredients with warm, not hot, milk.
3. Mix to a dough and knead for 10 minutes on a lightly floured surface or 1 minute in a food processor. Transfer to an oiled polythene bag and leave in a warm place until doubled in size.
4. Meanwhile fry the onion in the remaining butter without browning and leave to cool.
5. Knead the dough again for 2 minutes, then roll out into an oblong shape 36 × 20 cm (14 × 8 inches).
6. Spoon the onion on to the dough and scatter with the parsley. Brush the edges with water and roll up like a Swiss roll from the longest edge. Cut into 8 pieces and place carefully into an oiled 24 cm (9½ inch) round cake tin.
7. Leave to rise until doubled in size, then bake in a preheated oven for 10 minutes. Reduce the heat and cook for a further 25-30 minutes.

Roll up like a Swiss roll

Slice into 8 pieces

SAVOURY BUTTERS FOR GRILLED MEATS

Basic recipe:
100 g (4 oz) unsalted butter, softened
grated rind and juice of ½ lemon

Preparation time: 10 minutes

Variations:
Maître d'hôtel butter: Beat the butter and work in the lemon rind and juice together with 2 tablespoons finely chopped fresh parsley.
Garlic butter: Add 2 cloves garlic, peeled and crushed to the maître d'hôtel butter.
Tarragon butter: Add 2 tablespoons washed, dried and chopped leaves of tarragon to the basic recipe.
Chive butter: Omit the lemon rind and juice and add 1 teaspoon grated onion and 1-2 tablespoons chopped fresh chives to the basic recipe.
Mint butter: Blanch a handful, 15 g (½ oz), fresh mint leaves in boiling water for 30 seconds. Drain and dry on paper towels. Chop finely or crush in a pestle and mortar and add to the basic recipe.
Watercress butter: Prepare as for mint butter, using the leaves from 1 bunch of watercress.

Spoon the prepared butters on to a square of foil and form the parcel into a sausage shape. Seal the ends. Label and freeze. Slices can then be cut from the roll as and when required.

Use maître d'hôtel, tarragon or watercress butters for fish, chicken or veal.

Use garlic butter for steaks, chives or mint for lamb and pork.

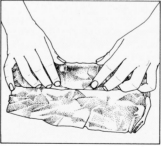
Spoon the butters into a square of foil. Roll up neatly into a sausage shape. Chill or freeze

Slices can be cut from the roll when required

From the left: Onion and parsley party loaf; Canadian chowder

CANADIAN CHOWDER

450 g (1 lb) cod or haddock fillet
salt
900 ml (1½ pints) water
450 g (1 lb) potatoes, peeled and diced
4 rashers lean belly of pork, skin removed and diced
1 medium onion, peeled and chopped
25 g (1 oz) butter
450 ml (¾ pint) milk
freshly ground black pepper
2 tablespoons chopped fresh parsley
2 tablespoons chopped fresh chives

Preparation time: 20 minutes
Cooking time: 40 minutes

1. Place the fish and salt in a large pan and cover with water. Bring to the boil, cover and cook gently for 10 minutes. Drain from the pan, skin and remove bones. Flake the fish and reserve.
2. Strain the cooking liquid into another pan, add the potato dice and extra water if necessary, cover and cook for 10-15 minutes until the potatoes are just tender.
3. Meanwhile, in a large pan fry the belly of pork and onion in the butter until just turning golden. Pour in the potato stock and enough milk to make a soup-like consistency. Cook for 10-15 minutes.
4. Add the reserved flaked fish, potato dice, salt, pepper, parsley and chives. Return to the boil. Serve in hot bowls with bread.

CHINESE FRIED RICE

450 g (1 lb) cold cooked rice (about 175 g (6 oz) before
   cooking)
salt
1 egg, beaten
6-8 tablespoons oil
8 shallots or 2 small onions, peeled and sliced
3 garlic cloves, peeled and crushed
100 g (4 oz) peeled prawns, thawed if frozen
100 g (4 oz) Chinese sausage, sliced (optional)
100 g (4 oz) cold roast pork, shredded (optional)
4 Chinese dried mushrooms, soaked in water for 1 hour,
   drained and sliced (optional)
1-2 tablespoons light soy sauce
freshly ground black pepper
100 g (4 oz) frozen peas, thawed
2 spring onions, trimmed, peeled and sliced
1 red chilli, trimmed, seeded and chopped (optional)
fresh coriander leaves (optional)
To garnish:
shredded lettuce leaves
bay leaves (optional)

Preparation time: 30 minutes, plus cooling
Cooking time: 12-15 minutes

The Chinese mushrooms and sausages are available in
Chinese stores and give an authentic flavour to this
recipe. There are two kinds of soy sauce: one is dark
and thick, like treacle, but the recipe uses the thin
"light" soy sauce.

1. Cook the rice in boiling salted water until tender.
Drain and leave to go cold or cool overnight.
2. In a frying pan cook the egg in a little of the oil to
make an omelette. Roll up into a sausage and cut into
fine strips. Reserve.
3. Stir-fry the shallots or onions in oil in a wok or large
frying pan until crisp and golden brown. Lift out and
reserve.
4. Heat the prawns and garlic for a minute and set
aside.
5. Fry the Chinese sausage, shredded pork and
mushrooms, lift out and reserve.
6. Stir-fry the rice in sufficient hot oil to coat the
grains, add the soy sauce, salt and pepper, plus half of
the reserved cooked ingredients. Mix well. Add the
peas and half the spring onion. Serve on a warmed
platter and finish with the remaining cooked ingredients, spring onion, chilli and coriander leaves (if
using). Surround the rice with a garnish of shredded
lettuce and bay leaves, if liked.

TONGUE WITH GINGERNUT SAUCE

1 medium size salted ox tongue, about 1.5 kg (3 lb), soaked
   in cold water overnight, drained
1 medium onion, peeled and quartered
1 carrot, peeled and sliced
bouquet garni (page 6)
Gingernut sauce:
1 medium onion, peeled and finely chopped
2 tablespoons oil
1 teaspoon ground ginger
50 g (2 oz) soft brown sugar
1 tablespoon golden syrup
6 gingernut biscuits, finely crushed
450 ml (¾ pint) stock from cooking the tongue
50 g (2 oz) sultanas
50 g (2 oz) raisins
1 orange
salt
freshly ground black pepper

**Preparation time: 30 minutes, plus soaking overnight
and standing
Cooking time: about 3½ hours
Oven: 180°C, 350°F, Gas Mark 5**

1. In a large pan cover the tongue with fresh water and
bring to the boil. Drain and cover again with more
water. Add the onion, carrot and bouquet garni and
bring to the boil. Cover and simmer gently for 3 hours.
2. Cool the tongue in the pan for about an hour, so that
it will be easier to handle. Strain and reserve 450 ml
(¾ pint) of the cooking liquid.
3. Meanwhile prepare the sauce by frying the onion in
the oil in a large frying pan for about 2 minutes. Add
the ground ginger, brown sugar, golden syrup and ginger biscuits. Stir in the reserved stock, sultanas and
raisins, the juice of half the orange, salt and pepper.
4. Carefully lift the tongue on to a board. Remove the
bones from the root of the tongue and strip off the skin.
Slice the tongue and place in a shallow ovenproof
dish. Pour over the prepared sauce. Cover with foil and
reheat in a preheated oven for 10-15 minutes.
5. Serve garnished with the remaining orange half, cut
into slices. Any tongue left over can be cooled, covered
and stored in the refrigerator.

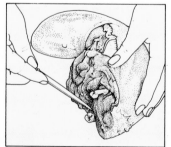
Remove bones from the root

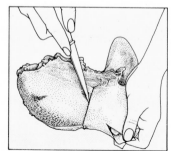
Peel off skin with knife

SQUID WITH PINEAPPLE AND GINGER

750 g (1½ lb) fresh or frozen squid, thawed if frozen
3 tablespoons oyster sauce
freshly ground black pepper
2.5 cm (1 inch) piece of fresh ginger, scraped and crushed
1 × 350 g (12 oz) can pineapple pieces, drained, or the
   same weight in fresh pineapple pieces
6 spring onions, trimmed and peeled
6 tablespoons oil
1-2 teaspoons cornflour mixed to a paste with a little of the
   pineapple juice

**Preparation time: 30 minutes, plus standing
Cooking time: 10 minutes**

1. Remove the head and tentacles from the pocket of
each squid. Remove the purplish skin from the outside. Discard the eyes and the hard core in the centre of
the tentacles. Reserve the tentacles.
2. Pull out the transparent bone from the pocket and
slit the squid from top to bottom, open up and wash
well.
3. Flatten the squid inside uppermost. Using a sharp
knife lightly score a lattice pattern in the flesh being
careful not to cut right through. Cut the squid into 3
ribbon-like pieces from top to base.
4. Place in a bowl with the tentacles, oyster sauce,
pepper and ginger. Stand for 10 minutes, stirring occasionally.
5. Place the pineapple in a small bowl. Cut the white
part off the spring onions and cut the green tops into
5 cm (2 inch) lengths. Heat the oil in a wok and fry the
white parts of the spring onions until just coloured.
Add the drained squid, reserving the marinade. Stir
over a brisk heat, so that the squid curls. Cook for 4-5
minutes only. Using a slotted draining spoon, lift the
squid on to a hot serving dish and keep warm.
6. Pour the reserved marinade into the wok, remove
the piece of ginger and add the pineapple pieces. Cook
for 1 minute.
7. Stir in the blended cornflour and cook until the
sauce thickens. Return the squid and heat through. At
the last minute stir in the spring onion tops. Taste and
adjust the seasoning and serve immediately, accompanied by freshly boiled rice.

Remove head and purplish skin

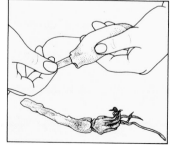
Pull out transparent bone

LIVER WITH SAGE
COOKED CHINESE STYLE

2 medium carrots, peeled and sliced
350 g (12 oz) fresh calves' liver
2 tablespoons seasoned cornflour (page 26)
4 tablespoons oil
1 tablespoon soy sauce
1 tablespoon Chinese rice wine or sherry
few sprigs fresh sage, leaves only, or 1 teaspoon dried sage
50 ml (2 fl oz) stock or water
salt
freshly ground black pepper
2 teaspoons sesame oil
few sprigs of sage, to garnish

Preparation time: 15 minutes
Cooking time: 8-10 minutes

1. Blanch the carrots in fast boiling water for 4 minutes. Drain.
2. Rinse and dry the liver, then cut into finger size pieces. Toss in the seasoned cornflour.
3. Fry in hot oil until the liver changes colour, stirring constantly, then cook for a further 2-3 minutes over a gentle heat. Using a slotted draining spoon, lift on to a dish and keep hot.
4. Add the soy sauce, rice wine or sherry, sage and stock to the juices in the pan. Cook uncovered to reduce the sauce to a little, stirring frequently.
5. Taste and adjust the seasoning. Return the liver to the pan for a minute, then stir in most of the carrots and sesame oil.
6. Serve garnished with the remaining carrots and sprigs of fresh sage.

From the left: Tongue with gingernut sauce; Squid with pineapple and ginger; Liver and sage cooked Chinese style; sage

BAKED MACKEREL WITH ROSEMARY

4 medium size mackerel, cleaned, heads and tails left on
15 g (½ oz) butter
4 sprigs of rosemary
salt
freshly ground black pepper
1 lemon, to garnish

Preparation time: 5 minutes
Cooking time: 30 minutes
Oven: 200°C, 400°F, Gas Mark 6

1. Wash the fish and wipe dry using paper towels. Make 3 slashes on each side with a sharp knife and lay the fish side by side in a buttered shallow ovenproof dish.
2. Nip the top part from each rosemary sprig and reserve for garnish. Place the rest of the sprig into the gut of each fish. Season with salt and pepper.
3. Bake in a preheated oven for 30 minutes or until the fish is tender and browned.
4. Remove the sprigs of rosemary and serve garnished with the rosemary tops and wedges of lemon. Creamed horseradish is delicious served with mackerel.

KEDGEREE

450 g (1 lb) smoked haddock
50 g (2 oz) butter
6 tablespoons oil
1 small onion, peeled and finely chopped
1 cm (½ inch) piece of fresh ginger, scraped and sliced, then shredded
1 red chilli, trimmed, seeded and sliced into rings
225 g (8 oz) basmatti rice washed and soaked for 30 minutes in cold water, drained
½ teaspoon ground turmeric (optional)
2 whole cloves
salt
freshly ground black pepper
To garnish:
1 large onion, peeled, sliced and dried on paper towels
2 hard-boiled eggs, halved
1 tablespoon chopped fresh parsley
sprigs of oregano

Preparation time: 20 minutes, plus soaking
Cooking time: 30 minutes

1. Place the haddock in a shallow pan with sufficient water to cover. Bring to the boil, cover and cook over a gentle heat for 8-10 minutes only.
2. Meanwhile heat 25 g (1 oz) of the butter and 1 tablespoon of the oil in a pan. Add the onion, ginger and chilli, then the rice. Stir until the grains are coated with oil. Add the turmeric, if using, then the cloves.
3. Strain the cooking liquid from the fish and stir 600 ml (1 pint) into the rice. Season with salt and pepper. Bring to the boil, cover and cook over a gentle heat for 10-15 minutes or until all the liquid has been absorbed and the rice is tender.
4. Flake the fish and add to the rice with the remaining butter and heat thoroughly.
5. Fry the onion in the remaining oil until crisp and golden. Serve the kedgeree garnished with the halved hard-boiled eggs, onion rings, sprinkle with chopped parsley and sprigs of oregano.

SKATE WITH BLACK BUTTER

1 wing of skate, about 750 g (1½ lb)
1 small onion, peeled and sliced
1 bay leaf
2 sprigs of parsley
salt
a few whole black peppercorns
2-3 tablespoons herb or cider vinegar
1 tablespoon chopped fresh parsley
1 tablespoon capers
Sauce:
50 g (2 oz) butter
salt
freshly ground black pepper
2 tablespoons herb or cider vinegar

Preparation time: 10 minutes
Cooking time: 40 minutes

1. Place the fish in a large pan and cover with water. Add the onion, bay leaf, parsley, salt, peppercorns and vinegar and bring to the boil. Reduce the heat and simmer uncovered for about 20 minutes.
2. Using a slotted fish slice, drain the fish and place on a board or dish lined with paper towels. Remove any skin from both sides and divide the fish into portions.
3. Transfer to a large ovenproof dish, sprinkle with the parsley and capers. Cover with foil and keep hot.
4. To make the sauce, heat the butter in a pan and allow to foam and slightly brown. Pour immediately over the fish and sprinkle with salt and pepper.
5. Pour the vinegar into the pan in which the butter was browned, boil and pour over the fish. Serve immediately.

From the top: Skate with black butter; oregano; sorrel; Fish pie with sorrel; Kedgeree

FISH PIE WITH SORREL

450 g (1 lb) cod or haddock fillet, skinned
350 ml (12 fl oz) milk
salt
freshly ground black pepper
50 g (2 oz) butter or margarine
40 g (1½ oz) plain flour
3-4 tablespoons single or whipping cream
100 g (4 oz) peeled prawns, thawed if frozen
100 g (4 oz) fresh sorrel, washed and dried
200 g (8 oz) prepared puff pastry, thawed if frozen
1 egg, beaten, or milk

Preparation time: 45 minutes, plus resting
Cooking time: 25-30 minutes
Oven: 230°C, 450°F, Gas Mark 8;
**   190°C, 375°F, Gas Mark 5**

Sorrel gives an unusual, tart flavour to this fish pie, which compliments the rich sauce. It grows from spring until November and is wonderful incorporated in salads and omelettes. Use an equal quantity of spinach, when sorrel is not available and add a tablespoon of lemon juice.

1. Poach the fish in a large pan with the milk, salt and pepper for 5-8 minutes. Strain the cooking liquid and reserve.
2. Using a slotted fish slice, lift the fish on to a plate. Discard any bones, flake the fish and reserve.
3. Melt 40 g (1½ oz) of the butter or margarine in another pan, add the flour and mix well. Cook over a gentle heat for 1 minute. Away from the heat, stir in the cooking liquid until thoroughly blended. Return to the heat and stir constantly until the sauce is smooth and thickens. Cool, then add the cream, prawns and flaked fish.
4. Discard the centre stem of the sorrel leaves and roll the leaves into a parcel. Shred with scissors or a sharp knife and cook in the remaining butter or margarine until softened.
5. Roll out the pastry to 3 mm (⅛ inch) thick. Invert a 900 ml (1½ pint) pie dish on the pastry and cut out the lid. Cut a strip of pastry from the trimmings to line the wetted rim of the pie dish. Place a pie funnel in the centre of the dish then fill with the fish sauce and sorrel.
6. Dampen the pastry covering the rim and place the pastry lid in position. Decorate the pastry edges. Make a small hole in the centre and decorate with any pastry trimmings.
7. Rest the pie in the refrigerator for 30 minutes.
8. Brush with beaten egg or milk and bake in a preheated oven for 10 minutes, then reduce the oven temperature and cook for a further 15-20 minutes, until the pastry is golden brown.

IMPRESSIVE DISHES

CROWN ROAST OF LAMB WITH LEMON AND MINT STUFFING

Serves 6
1 crown roast lamb, about 1.25 kg (2½ lb)
50 g (2 oz) butter, melted
salt
freshly ground black pepper
Stuffing balls:
175 g (6 oz) fresh white breadcrumbs
finely grated rind and juice of 1 lemon
2-3 tablespoons finely chopped fresh mint
2 eggs, beaten
salt
freshly ground black pepper
sprigs of mint, to garnish

Preparation time: 15 minutes
Cooking time: about 1-1½ hours
Oven: 230°C, 450°F, Gas Mark 8;
       180°C, 350°F, Gas Mark 4

The crown is made from 2 matching best ends of neck, with 6 to 8 bones in each. The best ends are chined, then tied together skin side facing inwards to form a crown. The tips of the bones are scraped clean and each covered with a small double square of foil to prevent burning whilst cooking.

1. Brush the crown roast with half the melted butter and season with salt and pepper. Place on a rack in a roasting tin. Make a firm ball of foil and press into the centre cavity.
2. Place in a preheated oven for 10 minutes to seal the meat, then reduce the temperature and cook for a further ¾-1¼ hours. Test with a skewer to see whether the meat is done to your liking.
3. Meanwhile prepare the stuffing. Mix the breadcrumbs, lemon rind and juice and mint together. Add the remaining melted butter and sufficient egg to bind. Season with salt and pepper to taste. Roll into balls about the size of a walnut and place in the base of the meat tin after the first 30 minutes' cooking. Baste with a little of the fat.
4. When the meat is cooked, lift on to a serving dish and leave in a warm place for 5-10 minutes.
5. Remove the silver foil caps from the bones and replace with cutlet frills. Lift the foil ball from the centre and fill with the stuffing balls. Garnish with the mint leaves and serve.

BEEF OLIVES

Serves 8
8 thin slices of silverside of beef, about 100-150 g (4-5 oz) each
100 g (4 oz) fresh breadcrumbs
50 g (2 oz) chopped suet
2 teaspoons chopped fresh parsley
1 teaspoon chopped fresh oregano
1 teaspoon chopped fresh thyme
salt
freshly ground black pepper
1 egg (size 1, 2)
40 g (1½ oz) seasoned flour (page 26)
4-6 tablespoons oil
1 large onion, peeled and chopped
900 ml (1½ pints) beef stock or stock cube and water
2 tablespoons tomato purée
3 tablespoons red wine
freshly chopped parsley, to garnish

Preparation time: 30 minutes
Cooking time: 2½ hours
Oven: 180°C, 350°F, Gas Mark 4

1. Trim the beef slices if necessary. Mix the breadcrumbs, suet, chopped herbs, salt and pepper with sufficient beaten egg to bind.
2. Spoon the mixture equally on to the beef slices, roll each one up into a neat parcel and tie with fine string or strong thread.
3. Toss lightly in seasoned flour, then fry in hot oil and brown all over. Lift out of the pan.
4. Fry the onion in the remaining oil until soft. Add the remaining seasoned flour and cook for a minute stirring constantly. Away from the heat, stir in the stock, tomato purée and wine. Return to the heat and bring to the boil, stirring constantly. Taste and adjust the seasoning.
5. Return the beef olives to the pan or transfer the beef and liquid to an ovenproof casserole. Cover and cook for about 1½-2 hours or in a preheated oven until the meat is tender.
6. Serve on a hot serving dish with freshly cooked carrots or broccoli, mashed potatoes and sprinkled with parsley.

From the back: Crown roast of lamb
with lemon and mint stuffing; Beef olives

CHICKEN RENDANG

1½ kg (3 lb) fresh chicken, skinned and jointed into
    8 pieces
1 teaspoon sugar
350 g (12 oz) desiccated coconut
450 ml (¾ pint) boiling water
4 small red or white onions, peeled
2 garlic cloves, peeled and crushed
2.5 cm (1 inch) piece of fresh ginger
1-2 stems of lemon grass, serai powder, or a few strips of
    lemon rind
5 tablespoons coconut or vegetable oil
2-4 teaspoons chilli powder
piece dried laos root or 1 level teaspoon laos powder
    (optional)
2 teaspoons salt or to taste

Preparation time: 1 hour 20 minutes
Cooking time: 50 minutes
Oven: 190°C, 375°F, Gas Mark 5

1. Sprinkle the chicken pieces with the sugar and leave to stand.
2. Dry-fry 75 g (3 oz) of the coconut. Transfer to a food processor or blender and process until the coconut becomes an oily paste. Scrape into a dish and reserve.
3. Place the remaining coconut in the blender or processor with the boiling water. Process for 30 seconds, then transfer to a separate bowl and cool to hand temperature. Strain and squeeze the coconut through a sieve over a bowl to produce approximately 300 ml (½ pint) coconut milk. Leave to stand for a few minutes, until the cream has risen to the surface.
4. Meanwhile blend the onions, garlic, ginger and the lower 5 cm (2 inch) stem of lemon grass or serai powder or lemon rind to a paste.
5. Heat the oil in a large saucepan or wok and fry the onion mixture for a few minutes. Reduce the heat, then stir in the chilli powder (according to taste) and laos root or powder (if using). Cook for 2-3 minutes stirring constantly.
6. Spoon in 4 tablespoons of the coconut cream from the milk and add salt to taste. When bubbling, add the chicken joints, turning them until they are well coated with the spices.
7. Pour in the remaining coconut milk, stirring constantly to prevent curdling. Add the top part of the stems of lemon grass. Cover and cook gently for 40-45 minutes until the chicken pieces are tender.
8. A few minutes before serving, stir in the dry-fried coconut to thicken the sauce. Bring to the boil, then simmer for 5 minutes. Remove the lemon grass.
9. Serve with freshly boiled rice, deep fried anchovy fish, Acar, prawn crackers, pickles or chutneys.

ACAR

100 g (4 oz) fresh peanuts or roasted salted peanuts
4 macadamia nuts or almonds, blanched and skinned
3 small onions, peeled
2 garlic cloves, peeled and crushed
5 tablespoons oil
1½ tablespoons ground turmeric
450 ml (¾ pint) white vinegar
4 tablespoons sugar
salt
a selection of vegetables and fruits to make up a total of 750 g
    (1½ lb) e.g. carrot, sliced; cauliflower, broken into small
    florets; cabbage, shredded; cucumber, sliced; small
    onions, left whole; green mango, sliced; fresh pineapple,
    cubed; 1 green chilli, trimmed, seeded and finely
    chopped; 1 red chilli, trimmed, seeded and finely
    chopped

Preparation time: 30 minutes
Cooking time: 10 minutes
Oven: 200°C, 400°F, Gas Mark 6

This vegetable pickle (pronounced 'acha') is the Malaysian version of piccalilli. It is often served with curries, though it also compliments cold meats and some fish dishes. If you use salted peanuts be sure to be discreet with the amount of salt used in the recipe.

1. If using fresh peanuts, roast on a baking tray in a preheated oven till brown, about 10 minutes.
2. Turn into a clean teatowel, then fold up and rub the nuts vigorously to remove the skins. Grind lightly without reducing them to a paste. Keep the nuts on one side.
3. Pound the macadamia nuts or almonds in a pestle and mortar or blender and reserve.
4. Pound the onions and garlic to a paste. Heat the oil and fry the onion mixture for 2-3 minutes. Add the macadamia or almonds and turmeric. Stir in the vinegar and sugar and a little salt to taste.
5. Add the prepared vegetables and fruits. Cook briefly for 2 minutes, turning all the time.
6. Add the peanuts to the mixture and leave to cool.
7. Transfer to two 900 g (2 lb) screwtop glass jars, seal and store in a cool place or refrigerator. The Acar will keep up to a month.

From the top: Chicken satay; Acar; Chicken rendang;
prawn crackers; deep fried anchovy fish

CHICKEN SATAY

4 chicken breasts, boned, unskinned, and cut into 1 cm
(½ inch) cubes
1 teaspoon brown sugar
18-20 bamboo or coconut skewers, soaked in water for at
least 2 hours
Marinade:
½ teaspoon cumin seeds
½ teaspoon fennel seeds
½ teaspoon coriander seeds
6 shallots or small onions, peeled and sliced
1 garlic clove, peeled and crushed
1 stem lemon grass, trimmed, lower 5 cm (2 inches) sliced
3 macadamia or cashew nuts
½ teaspoon ground turmeric
Peanut sauce:
100 g (4 oz) fresh peanuts, roasted
4 shallots or small onions, peeled and sliced
2 garlic cloves, peeled and crushed
1 cm (½ inch) cube prepared blachan (page 9)
6 macadamia or cashew nuts or almonds
2 stems lemon grass, trimmed, lower 5 cm (2 inches), sliced
3 tablespoons coconut or peanut oil
2-3 teaspoons chilli powder
300 ml (½ pint) coconut milk (page 9)
4-5 tablespoons tamarind water (page 67)
1 tablespoon brown sugar
salt

Preparation time: 45 minutes, plus marinating
Cooking time: 16-18 minutes

1. Sprinkle the chicken with the brown sugar.
2. To make the marinade, dry-fry the spices over a
medium heat, then grind to a powder.
3. Pound the shallots or onions, garlic, sliced lemon
grass and nuts to a paste, and mix the paste with the
spices and turmeric. Add the chicken pieces and coat
with the mixture. Marinate at least 4 hours. Then
thread on to the skewers.
4. To make the sauce, grind the peanuts until coarse
and still gritty. Reserve.
5. Pound or process the onions with the garlic and
blachan. Add the cashew nuts and the lower stems of
lemon grass. Process to a fine purée.
6. Fry this mixture in the hot oil for 2-3 minutes. Add
the chilli powder and cook for 2 minutes.
7. Stir in the coconut milk and bring to the boil. Reduce the heat and add the tamarind water, sugar, salt
and ground peanuts and cook until the sauce thickens.
8. To cook the satay, place the skewers of chicken over
a barbecue or under a preheated grill. Brush the chicken with a little coconut or peanut oil. Cook until golden and tender.
9. Serve on a large platter with chunks of cucumber
and onion, accompanied by the hot peanut sauce.

ITALIAN FISH SALAD

Serves 6 as a main course
Serves 12 as part of a buffet
1 kg (2 lb) squid, thawed if frozen
225 g (8 oz) Queen scallops, thawed if frozen
1½ kg (3 lb) mussels, scrubbed with beards removed
3 tablespoons oil
1 garlic clove, peeled and crushed
150 ml (¼ pint) white wine or water
juice of 1 large lemon (60 ml/2 fl oz)
150 ml (¼ pint) olive oil
1 teaspoon sugar
salt
freshly ground black pepper
200 g (8 oz) peeled prawns, thawed if frozen
1 head celery
2 tablespoons chopped fresh parsley
1 red pepper, cored, seeded and cut into strips
1 green pepper, cored, seeded and cut into strips
few lettuce leaves

Preparation time: 1 hour, plus soaking and cooling
Cooking time: 8-10 minutes

1. Prepare the squid as on page 42 and leave to dry on paper towels together with the scallops. Soak the mussels in cold water for about 1 hour, drain, then discard any which are open.
2. Heat the oil and add the garlic, then fry the squid, turning all the time until it curls. Add the scallops, cover and cook gently for 3-4 minutes only, turning frequently. Using a slotted draining spoon lift the contents of the pan on to a plate and leave until cold.
3. Meanwhile, cook the mussels in the wine or boiling water in a covered heavy pan until they open. Discard any mussels that fail to open. Cool for a few minutes. Reserve a few mussels in their shells for garnish, then remove the remainder from their shells. Leave until completely cold.
4. Blend the lemon juice, oil, sugar and salt and pepper together. Pour over the cold squid, scallops, mussels and prawns. Toss together and stand for at least 1 hour stirring occasionally.
5. Remove the outer sticks from the celery. Reserve some of the leaves for garnish and chop the remainder. Toss with the prepared peppers, and some of the parsley and mix well.
6. Combine the fish, celery and peppers and arrange on a bed of lettuce. Garnish with the reserved mussel shells round the edge of the platter, celery leaves and remaining parsley on top. Serve with plenty of French bread. Small portions are also delicious as a starter.

GREEK CHICKEN WITH LEMON SAUCE

1.5 kg (3½ lb) fresh chicken
1 carrot, peeled and sliced
1 large onion, peeled and sliced
few sprigs of thyme
salt
½ teaspoon black peppercorns
4 tablespoons lemon juice
275 g (10 oz) long-grain rice
300 ml (½ pint) whipping cream
2 egg yolks
freshly ground white or black pepper
To garnish:
50 g (2 oz) broken walnuts
50 g (2 oz) black olives
sprigs of fresh herbs

Preparation time: 30 minutes, plus cooling
Cooking time: 1¼-1¾ hours

1. Wipe the chicken, then place in a large pan with the carrot, onion, thyme, salt, peppercorns and sufficient water barely to cover the bird. Bring to the boil, cover and simmer for 1-1½ hours, until the chicken is tender. Skim if necessary.
2. Cool in the liquid then lift out, skin and divide the chicken meat into bite-size pieces.
3. Boil 600 ml (1 pint) of the skimmed stock rapidly and reduce by half, reserving the remainder. Allow to cool and add the lemon juice.
4. Meanwhile, boil the remaining stock and add the rice. Cook until tender. Drain and cool.
5. Beat the cream and egg yolks, add a little of the warm stock, pour the cream mixture into a pan over gentle heat and stir until the sauce thickens. Do not boil or the sauce will curdle.
6. Taste and adjust the seasoning and stir the chicken pieces into the sauce. Leave to cool until the sauce coats the chicken, about 30 minutes.
7. To serve, spoon the rice on to a serving platter. Arrange the chicken and sauce on top. Cover and chill.
8. Just before serving, garnish with the walnuts, olives and herbs.

Garnish dishes with fresh herbs just before serving. Fresh herbs will rapidly deteriorate once placed on food. Sprigs of fresh herbs are best stored in a plastic bag at the bottom of the refrigerator and will last for about a week. Alternatively, they can be stored standing in a jar of water and loosely covered with a plastic bag. Refresh the water regularly.

From the left: Italian fish salad;
Greek chicken with lemon sauce

ITALIAN LAYERED SOUFFLÉ

50 g (2 oz) pasta shells or small macaroni
salt
1 tablespoon chopped fresh basil, marjoram or parsley
Soufflé:
50 g (2 oz) butter
50 g (2 oz) grated Parmesan cheese
40 g (1½ oz) plain flour
450 ml (¾ pint) milk
freshly ground black pepper
3 eggs, separated
1 large beefsteak tomato, peeled and thinly sliced

Preparation time: 35 minutes
Cooking time: 25-30 minutes
Oven: 190°C, 375°F, Gas Mark 5

1. Boil the pasta in salted water until tender. Rinse, drain, then mix with the herbs and reserve.
2. Butter a 1.5 litre (2½ pint) soufflé dish with 15 g (½ oz) of the butter and coat the sides generously with about a third of the Parmesan cheese.
3. Melt the remaining butter, then stir in the flour to make a roux. Cook over a gentle heat for 30 seconds. Away from the heat, stir in the milk. Return to the heat, stirring constantly until the sauce is smooth and thick.
4. Remove from the heat and cool. Season with salt and pepper and beat in the egg yolks. Whisk the egg whites until firm, then fold into the sauce.
5. Pour one-third of the mixture into the prepared dish. Cover with half the pasta, the tomato slices and half the remaining cheese. Spoon one-third of the soufflé mixture into the remaining pasta mix and pour into the soufflé dish. Top with the remaining soufflé mixture and cheese.
6. Place on a baking sheet and cook in a preheated oven for 25-30 minutes until well risen. Serve hot.

COLD CURRIED PARTY CHICKEN

Serves 8-10

2 × 1.5 kg (3 lb) fresh chicken, with giblets
salt
freshly ground black pepper
1 carrot, peeled and quartered
1 celery stick, roughly chopped
bouquet garni (page 6)
450 g (1 lb) long grain rice
Sauce:
4 tablespoons oil
2 medium onions, peeled and finely chopped
2 tablespoons hot or mild curry powder (page 16)
300 ml (½ pint) red or white wine
150 ml (¼ pint) stock, strained
1 × 411 g (14½ oz) can apricot halves, drained
600 ml (1 pint) mayonnaise
juice of 1 large lemon
150 ml (¼ pint) whipping cream, whipped
To garnish:
100 g (4 oz) flaked almonds, toasted
sprigs of fresh coriander or parsley

Preparation time: 50 minutes
Cooking time: 1¼ hours

1. Rinse and wipe the chickens, then place in a large saucepan or 2 medium size saucepans with the giblets, sufficient water just to cover, salt and pepper, carrot, celery and bouquet garni. Bring to the boil, cover and simmer for 1 hour until just tender.
2. Cool the chicken in the liquid. Lift out and remove the meat from the bones and reserve.
3. Keep aside 150 ml (¼ pint) stock for the sauce. Place 1.2 litres (2 pints) of the remaining stock in a saucepan, add the rice and cook until tender. (The remainder of the stock could be frozen in small containers for future use.) Allow the rice to cool.
4. To make the sauce, heat the oil, and fry the onion until transparent. Add the curry powder and cook for 2 minutes stirring constantly.
5. Add the wine, stock and salt and pepper to taste. Cook uncovered, stirring occasionally, for 10 minutes, then blend or process until smooth. Strain and cool.
6. Purée 8 of the apricot halves and stir into the sauce. Place the remainder on paper towels, for garnish.
7. Stir the sauce into the mayonnaise. Add the lemon juice and adjust seasoning if necessary.
8. Fold in the whipped cream and then the chicken meat. Turn into the centre of a bed of rice and garnish with the apricot halves, toasted almonds and sprigs of fresh coriander or parsley.

MIDDLE EASTERN PICNIC CHICKEN

Serves 8

1 × 1.75 kg (3½ lb) chicken
2 tablespoons oil
1 tablespoon lemon juice
½ teaspoon ground turmeric
salt
freshly ground black pepper
85 ml (3 fl oz) water
200 g (7 oz) chicken livers, thawed if frozen
50 g (2 oz) butter
1 teaspoon tomato purée
2 tablespoons brandy
2 tablespoons single cream
2-3 tablespoons chopped mixed fresh herbs, mint, parsley, tarragon
grated rind and juice of ½ lemon
50 g (2 oz) pistachio nuts, roughly chopped
1 large sesame loaf – cottage shape, without the topknot, about 22 cm (9 inch) diameter

Preparation time: 40 minutes, plus cooling
Cooking time: about 1½-1¾ hours

1. Wipe the chicken with paper towels. Heat the oil in a deep pan or flameproof casserole with the lemon juice and turmeric. Place the chicken in the pan and turn over several times so that the chicken is coloured all over. Season with salt and pepper.

2. Reduce the heat, cover and cook gently for 30 minutes. Add the water, turn the chicken over again, then cook for a further ¾-1 hour or until tender.

3. Cool the chicken in the pan. Skim off the fat and reserve the chicken juices.

4. Remove the cooked chicken meat from the bones and cut into bite-size pieces.

5. Rinse and dry the chicken livers on paper towels. Fry in hot butter until they change colour. Add the tomato purée, cover and cook gently for 5-8 minutes or until tender. Cool, then add the brandy, cream and salt and pepper to taste. Purée in a blender or food processor until completely smooth.

6. Stir the herbs, lemon rind, juice, nuts and all the stock from the cooked chicken into the chicken pieces.

7. Cut a slice from the top of the loaf then scoop out all the soft bread from the base and lid. (Make breadcrumbs and store for future use.)

8. Spoon half the chicken mixture into the hollow base of the loaf, cover with the chicken liver mixture and fill up with the remaining chicken. Top with the lid and press down gently.

9. Cover closely with cling film and chill for several hours or overnight before serving.

10. Arrange on a board and cut into wedges like a cake to serve.

Scoop the soft bread from the base of the loaf

Spoon layers into hollowed-out loaf, pressing down well

From the left: Cold curried party chicken; Middle Eastern picnic chicken

SPINACH AND PORK TERRINE WITH GREEN PEPPERCORNS

Serves 6 as a main course
Serves 12 as part of a buffet
450 g (1 lb) fresh spinach, well washed, or 1 × 250 g (9 oz)
    packet frozen spinach
8 rashers streaky bacon, rinded
350 g (12 oz) lean belly of pork, boned, rinded and diced
450 g (1 lb) sausage meat
1 medium onion, peeled and finely chopped
2 garlic cloves, peeled and crushed
2 eggs
salt
freshly ground black pepper
½ teaspoon ground nutmeg
175-200 g (6-7 oz) sliced cooked ham, cut into finger-size
    pieces
2 tablespoons fresh whole or canned green peppercorns
1 bunch watercress, to garnish

Preparation time: 45 minutes
Cooking time: 1¼-1½ hours
Oven: 190°C, 375°F, Gas Mark 5

This terrine can be served hot with tiny new potatoes and a salad or cold as part of a buffet or for an after-theatre supper.

1. In a covered pan cook the spinach in the rinsing water left on the leaves until tender, or cook the frozen spinach as directed. Drain thoroughly.
2. Line a 1.6 litre (2¾ pint) terrine with the bacon.
3. Mince the belly of pork or chop finely in a food processor. Add the sausage meat then work in the onion, garlic, egg, salt and pepper and nutmeg.
4. Add the fresh cooked or prepared frozen spinach but do not overmix. Spoon half the prepared mixture into the lined terrine. Cover with pieces of the ham and peppercorns, then spoon in the remaining mixture. Smooth the top.
5. Place the terrine in a roasting tin with water to come one-third of the way up the sides of the dish.
6. Place in a preheated oven and cook for 1¼-1½ hours. When the terrine begins shrinking from the sides of the dish and a skewer inserted into the centre of the terrine is hot when removed, lift out of the water bath.
7. To serve cold, cover the terrine in the dish with greaseproof paper. Rest a plate and a heavy weight on top and leave in a cool place for several hours. Some of the juices will be reabsorbed and the rest will form a jelly. Turn out on to a dish and garnish with plenty of watercress.
8. Serve with the home-made Onion and parsley party loaf (page 38) and a green salad.

CHICKEN BREASTS WITH HERB AND GARLIC CHEESE

Serves 8 on a picnic
Serves 16 as part of a buffet
8 chicken breasts 125 g (5-6 oz) each, boned and skinned
1 × 150 g (5 oz) packet herb and garlic cream cheese
50 g (2 oz) seasoned flour (page 26)
2 eggs, beaten
125 g (6 oz) fresh breadcrumbs
oil for deep frying, or 1½ oz (40 g) butter for baking
To garnish:
225 g (8 oz) French beans, cooked but crunchy
12 black olives

Preparation time: 1 hour
Cooking time: 35-40 minutes
Oven: 190°C, 375°F, Gas Mark 5

Take them on a picnic or serve them as part of a buffet. Delicious served either hot or cold.

1. Slice each breast through to make 2 equal fillets. Place in pairs between sheets of damp greaseproof paper and beat with a rolling pin into thin escalopes.
2. Divide the cheese equally between each escalope and roll up neatly into a sausage shape. (The escalope will stay rolled up due to the dampness in the chicken breast.) Toss in the seasoned flour and dip in the egg and coat in breadcrumbs.
3. Deep fry several at a time in oil heated to 185°C, 360°F (or until a cube of bread browns in 3 seconds) for 8-10 minutes. Keep the cooked breasts warm whilst cooking the remainder. Drain on paper towels. Alternatively, arrange in a large buttered shallow ovenproof dish or roasting tin. Dot each one with a little butter and bake in a preheated oven for 35-40 minutes. Baste once or twice throughout cooking.
4. Serve on a bed of fluffy rice garnished with lightly cooked, crunchy French beans and black olives.

NOISETTES OF LAMB WITH HERB BUTTER

1 best end of lamb, about 1.25 kg (1½-2 lb)
25 g (1 oz) butter, melted
salt
freshly ground black pepper
50 g (2 oz) herb butter of your choice (page 38)
6 × 7½ cm (3 inch) circles of bread, fried
fresh herbs, to garnish

Preparation time: 5 minutes
Cooking time: 15-20 minutes

RATATOUILLE

2 aubergines, about 450 g (1 lb), cut into 5 mm (¼ inch) slices
350 g (12 oz) courgettes, cut into 5 mm (¼ inch) slices
salt
1 garlic clove, peeled and crushed
2 medium onions, peeled and sliced
150 ml (¼ pint) olive or cooking oil
1 green pepper, cored, seeded and cut into strips
1 red pepper, cored, seeded and cut into strips
3 large or 2 beefsteak tomatoes 450 g (1 lb), peeled and cut into chunky wedges
1 tablespoon chopped fresh basil
1 tablespoon chopped fresh parsley
freshly ground black pepper
grated Parmesan cheese, to serve

Preparation time: ½ hour
Cooking time: 30-40 minutes

This Mediterranean vegetable stew can be eaten either hot, warm or cold. For the latter make a day in advance and stand in a covered casserole in a cool place, not in the refrigerator. Serve as a starter, with roast meats or at a picnic with plenty of fresh bread. Try it with Carpet bag steaks too (page 57).

1. Spread the aubergine and courgette slices on a large plate and sprinkle with salt. Leave for 30 minutes, then rinse, drain and dry on paper towels.
2. Meanwhile, fry the garlic and onions in hot oil until soft and transparent.
3. Add the aubergine, courgettes and peppers to the pan. Mix carefully until the vegetables are coated in the oil. Cover and cook gently for 15-20 minutes, stirring occasionally.
4. Add the tomatoes, herbs and salt and pepper to taste. Cover and cook for a further 10-15 minutes until the vegetables are tender, but still retain their shape. Serve with grated Parmesan cheese.

Order the noisettes in advance. The best end of neck of lamb is chined, the chine bone and the rib bones are then removed. The meat is then rolled up from the thick end and tied neatly.

1. Brush the noisettes with melted butter, season with salt and pepper and place in a grill pan.
2. Cook under a preheated grill for 2 minutes on each side. Reduce the heat and cook for a further 10-12 minutes until the noisettes are tender.
3. Place a slice of the herb butter on each, then place the noisettes on the rounds of fried bread to serve. Garnish with fresh herbs.

CARPET BAG STEAKS

4 fillet or rump steaks, about 225-275 g (8-10 oz) each, and
    4 cm (1½ inch) thick
8 fresh oysters or 1 × 225 g (8 oz) can oysters in brine
1 lemon, halved
salt
freshly ground black pepper
50 g (2 oz) unsalted butter
2 tablespoons oil
2 tablespoons chopped fresh parsley

Preparation time: 15 minutes
Cooking time: 10-14 minutes

This recipe comes from Australia and is an inspired combination of some of their best raw ingredients cooked in a simple yet delicious way.

1. Slice each steak across to make a pocket without cutting completely through the meat.
2. Place 2 oysters in each pocket, with their juice if fresh, a squeeze of lemon juice from one half of the lemon and salt. Sew up the steaks with fine string or secure with wooden cocktail sticks.
3. Grind lots of black pepper on to the outside of each steak and pat down firmly.
4. Melt half the butter with the oil and fry the steaks for 1-2 minutes on each side, then cook for a further 6-8 minutes for rare, or 8-10 minutes for medium cooked steak. Transfer to a hot serving dish.
5. Add the remaining butter to the pan. When hot, stir in the parsley and pour immediately over the steaks. Garnish with the remaining lemon cut into wedges and eat immediately.
6. Serve with extra oysters if available.

Variation:
As an alternative, buy the meat in one whole piece rather than in individual steaks. It must be a thick cut. Cut through the centre to open up like a book. Fill with the oysters, lemon juice and salt and then stitch up with string. Cook a few minutes longer than for individual steaks depending on the rareness you prefer. Remove the string and cut into serving portions.

From the top: Ratatouille;
Chicken breasts with herb and garlic cheese

PORC AUX PRUNEAUX

Serves 6
175 g (6 oz) Californian prunes, pitted
450 ml (¾ pint) white wine
1 small cinnamon stick
4 whole cloves
1 kg (2 lb) pork fillet
40 g (1½ oz) seasoned flour (page 26)
50 g (2 oz) butter
1 tablespoon oil
3 tablespoons redcurrant jelly
300 ml (½ pint) soured cream, or double cream and
   2 tablespoons lemon juice
salt
freshly ground black pepper
To garnish:
lemon slices
few sprigs dill or fennel

Preparation time: 40 minutes, plus overnight soaking
Cooking time: 35-45 minutes
Oven: 150°C, 300°F, Gas Mark 2

Try sprinkling fresh feathery dill over fish, potato or pasta salads. Fennel looks similar to dill but has a strong aniseed flavour.

1. Soak the prunes in the wine overnight in an oven-proof casserole.
2. Strain off 50 ml (2 fl oz) of the wine and reserve. Add the cinnamon and cloves to the prunes then cover and cook the prunes in the remaining wine in a pre-heated oven for 30-40 minutes, or until plump.
3. Meanwhile, trim any skin from the pork fillets, then cut into noisettes about 5 cm (¼ inch) thick.
4. When the prunes are almost cooked, toss the noisettes in the seasoned flour, then fry in hot butter and oil for about 5 minutes on each side. Add the reserved wine to the noisettes in the pan, cover and cook for about 10 minutes.
5. Lift the pork and prunes on to a serving dish and keep warm.
6. Melt the redcurrant jelly in a pan, then add the wine in which the prunes have been cooked discarding the cinnamon and cloves. Whisk until smooth and allow to boil for 3-4 minutes to concentrate the flavour.
7. Add this liquid to the whisked cream, then pour the cream into the pan. Reheat without boiling. Taste and adjust the seasoning and pour over the pork and most of the prunes.
8. Arrange the remaining prunes round the dish and garnish with the lemon and sprigs of dill or fennel. Serve with freshly boiled rice.

SPICED BEEF

2.25 kg (5 lb) silverside of beef, tied securely
75 g (3 oz) light brown sugar
15 g (½ oz) saltpetre
100 g (4 oz) sea salt
25 g (1 oz) juniper berries
25 g (1 oz) black peppercorns
15 g (½ oz) allspice berries
300 ml (½ pint) water

Preparation time: 5 minutes on day 1; 10 minutes on day 3 and 1 minute daily for remainder
Cooking time: 4 hours
Oven: 140°C, 275°F, Gas Mark 1

Order the beef from the butcher a few days before you need it and buy the saltpetre from the chemist. This is a traditional recipe (not to be confused with salt beef) served in the stately homes and farms of old England. Forward planning is essential as it takes 12 days in all to prepare: 2 days in sugar, 9 days to marinate in spices, 1 day to cook, cool and weight down. It comes into its own over Christmas or if you have unexpected guests.

1. Wipe the beef and place in a large covered casserole. Smother with the brown sugar, cover and leave for 2 days in a very cool place or on the bottom shelf of the refrigerator. Spoon the juices which will collect over the meat and turn several times.
2. Crush the saltpetre, salt and spices together then rub on to the outside of the beef. Repeat the rubbing of the spices and juice into the beef at intervals for 9 days. Keep the meat covered in a cool place or base of the refrigerator.
3. To cook the beef, lightly rinse, then place with the water in an ovenproof casserole with a tightly fitting lid. You can use a sheet of foil or a double sheet of greaseproof paper between casserole and lid to ensure this. Cook in a preheated oven for just over 4 hours.
4. Remove from the oven and stand for 2-3 hours. Before the fatty liquid sets, lift the meat on to a double sheet of greaseproof paper on a board. Enclose into a neat parcel.
5. Sandwich the meat between plates and place a heavy weight on top. (Two 900 g (32 oz) cans of fruit or a clean brick wrapped in foil will do.) Leave for at least 24 hours before carving. Remove the string and serve in very thin slices with baked jacket potatoes and crisp crunchy salads.

Roast goose with sage, onion and apple stuffing;
cooked red cabbage

ROAST GOOSE WITH SAGE, ONION AND APPLE STUFFING

1 goose, about 3.5 kg (8 lb)
Stuffing:
750 g (1½ lb) eating apples
1 onion, peeled and finely chopped
100 g (4 oz) fresh breadcrumbs
1 tablespoon dried sage
salt
freshly ground black pepper
1 tablespoon flour
sprigs of fresh sage, to garnish

Preparation time: 15 minutes
Cooking time: about 3½ hours, plus standing
Oven: 200°C, 400°F, Gas Mark 6;
        190°C, 375°F, Gas Mark 5

The goose is regaining popularity, but it is still advisable to order in advance from your butcher.

1. Remove the excess fat from inside the goose. Prick the skin lightly, then set aside.
2. To make the stuffing, wash and quarter the apples. Remove the core but do not peel. Mix with the onion, breadcrumbs and sage. Season, then pile this mixture into the body cavity of the goose.
3. Sew up the opening with fine string and a trussing needle. Weigh the bird and calculate the cooking time, allowing 20 minutes per 450 g (1 lb) plus 20 minutes.
4. Season with salt and pepper, then place the goose in a roasting tin. Cook in a preheated oven for 30 minutes. Cover loosely with foil. Reduce the heat and cook for the rest of the calculated time.
5. Carefully pour off any excess fat half way through the cooking. About 45 minutes before the end of the cooking time, remove the foil and dust with the flour. Return to the oven to allow the breast to brown.
6. Allow to stand for 10 minutes in a warm place. The bird will then be easier to carve.
7. Cut the string so the apple stuffing can be served from the cavity with each helping. Garnish with sprigs of fresh sage and serve with red cabbage.

SOUTH AFRICAN PICKLED FISH

Serves 6-8 as a main course
Serves 12 as part of a buffet
1 kg (2¼ lb) haddock fillet, skinned
100 g (4 oz) seasoned flour (page 26)
2 eggs, beaten
oil, for shallow frying
Curry sauce:
450 ml (¾ pint) light malt vinegar
200 ml (⅓ pint) water
3 tablespoons brown sugar
3 teaspoons hot or mild curry powder (page 16)
1½ teaspoons ground turmeric
1 teaspoon plain flour
8 bay leaves
½ teaspoon salt
20 peppercorns
3-4 large onions, peeled and sliced
To garnish:
a few fresh bay leaves
1 red pepper, cored, seeded and cut into strips or rings
1 green pepper, cored, seeded and cut into strips or rings
1 lemon, sliced

Preparation time: 40 minutes, plus cooling
Cooking time: 15 minutes

This is a marvellous dish for a buffet – it should be cooked at least 2 days, or up to a week, ahead and requires very little last-minute attention. It is also a delicious and unusual way of serving up a humble and not so expensive fish.

1. Cut the fish into eight 7.5 × 5 cm (3 × 2 inch) pieces. Dip first in the seasoned flour, then quickly into the beaten egg, then back into the flour.
2. Fry on both sides in the oil until golden and just cooked. Drain on paper towels and repeat with the remaining fish.
3. Pour the vinegar, water and sugar into a pan. Stir over a low heat until the sugar dissolves. Blend a tablespoon of this liquid with the curry powder, turmeric and flour.
4. Away from the heat, stir the paste into the pan, then add the bay leaves, salt and peppercorns. Bring to the boil, stirring constantly, then add the onion slices. Cook for 5 minutes, then cool.
5. Place a layer of the fish in the base of a large casserole or suitable container. Cover with some onion and repeat in layers until all the fish and onions are used up. Pour over the sauce.
6. Cover with a lid or foil and leave in a cool place or the refrigerator for at least 2 days.
7. Garnish attractively with fresh bay leaves, red and green pepper and lemon slices. Serve with a rice salad, grated carrot, chutney and desiccated coconut.

SWEET AND SOUR WHOLE FISH

Serves 3
1 red snapper or fresh water bream, about 750 g (1½ lb), cleaned and scaled, head and tail left on, or a fillet of haddock
25 g (1 oz) seasoned cornflour (page 26)
oil, for shallow frying
Sauce:
2 tablespoons tomato ketchup
1 tablespoon sweet and sour sauce, or 1 tablespoon mango chutney and 1 teaspoon sugar
250 ml (8 fl oz) water
2 teaspoons cornflour
salt
freshly ground black pepper
3 tablespoons oil
1 small onion, peeled and cut into wedges
2 garlic cloves, peeled and crushed
½ green pepper, cored, seeded and cut into strips
1 tomato, peeled and cut into wedges
1 slice fresh pineapple cut into chunks or use part of a can of pineapple chunks, drained
1 red chilli, trimmed, seeded and cut into fine strips
2.5 cm (1 inch) piece of fresh ginger, scraped and cut into strips
To garnish:
fresh coriander leaves
spring onion curls (page 18)

Preparation time: 35 minutes
Cooking time: 15 minutes

A whole fish makes an impressive dish, however, as an alternative, cook individual steaks of fish to serve with the sauce.

1. Rinse and dry the fish on paper towels. Coat with the seasoned cornflour, then fry in hot oil for 5 minutes on each side. Lift carefully on to a hot serving plate and keep warm while preparing the sauce.
2. Blend the tomato ketchup with the sweet and sour sauce, or the mango chutney and sugar. Blend a little of the water with the cornflour, then add the remaining water and stir into the tomato mixture. Add salt and pepper to taste.
3. Heat the oil in a pan, fry the onion and garlic without browning, then add the pepper, tomato, fresh or canned pineapple. Stir well, then add the cornflour mixture, turning the fruit and vegetables until the sauce thickens. Add the chilli and ginger. Taste for sweetness and adjust the seasoning if necessary.
4. Pour over the cooked fish and garnish with fresh coriander leaves and spring onion curls.

From the left, clockwise: South African pickled fish;
Sweet and sour whole fish; Scallops with Béarnaise sauce

SCALLOPS ON SKEWERS WITH BÉARNAISE SAUCE

Makes 8 skewers – serves 2-4

8 fresh scallops
juice of 1 lemon or 60 ml (2 fl oz) dry white wine
½ teaspoon salt
8 rashers streaky bacon, rinded and cut in half
16 button mushrooms cooked in 25 g (1 oz) butter for
    1 minute
1 green pepper, seeded, cored and cut into chunks
a little olive oil
2 very small onions or shallots, peeled and finely chopped
4 tablespoons herb vinegar
2 tablespoons chopped fresh tarragon or ½ teaspoon dried
    tarragon
½ teaspoon mustard powder
4 egg yolks
100 g (4 oz) unsalted butter, melted
salt
freshly ground black pepper
lemon juice, to taste
2 teaspoons chopped fresh parsley

Preparation time: 45 minutes, plus marinating
Cooking time: 5-8 minutes

1. Remove the black thread from each scallop, cut away the coral and reserve. Cut each scallop in half. Marinate these in the lemon juice or wine and salt for at least 30 minutes.
2. Lift out on to paper towels, then wrap each scallop in a piece of bacon, which has been stretched with the flat surface of a blunt knife. Thread these on to the skewers alternately with the coral, mushrooms and green pepper. Brush with olive oil.
3. To make the sauce, place the onions or shallots in a small heavy pan with the vinegar and tarragon. Heat gently until the vinegar has reduced by half taking care not to burn the onion. Strain through a nylon sieve and reserve the liquid.
4. Place the mustard and egg yolks in a bowl over a pan of hot, not boiling, water and whisk until frothy. Add the strained vinegar mixture and then whisk in the butter in a thin stream. Add salt and pepper to taste. Sharpen with the lemon juice and stir in the parsley.
5. Keep the sauce warm by standing the bowl in a frying pan of bubbling water.
6. Place the skewers under a preheated grill and cook for a few minutes until the bacon is crisp.
7. Serve at once with the sauce.

BAKED SALMON WITH HERBS AND COLD WATERCRESS MAYONNAISE

Serves 10
1 whole salmon, about 2.25 kg (5 lb) gutted and cleaned, leaving head and tail on, or middle cut from a large fish
salt
freshly ground black pepper
a few sprigs of fresh herbs, e.g. dill, tarragon or parsley
1-2 tablespoons oil for cold fish
To garnish:
chopped fresh herb, e.g. dill, parsley
cucumber slices
lemon slices

Preparation time: 10 minutes, plus cooling
Cooking time: 1-1¼ hours
Oven: 150°C, 300°F, Gas Mark 2

Salmon is now much more readily available yet it still holds its reputation as a king of fish. For those who do not have a fish kettle, the answer is a foil parcel. Nothing could be easier yet more impressive than the whole baked salmon served cold.

1. Wipe the fish, season with salt and pepper inside and out, then stuff with the fresh herbs.
2. Cut a sheet of foil large enough to envelop the fish, then oil the foil. Make 2 strips of foil about 5 cm (2 inches) wide and about 30 cm (12 inches) long and place them 15 cm (6 inches) apart on the sheet of foil. Lift the fish on to them. (The strips will help lift the cooked fish later.) Lightly wrap the tail of the fish in an extra piece of foil to protect it while cooking.
3. Enclose the fish in a loose parcel, sealing the sides and ends and place in a large roasting tin or on a baking sheet.
4. Cook in a preheated oven allowing 10 minutes per 450 g (1 lb) plus 10 minutes. A larger fish may need 12 minutes per 450 g (1 lb) and 12 minutes over. Individual steaks 2.5 cm (1 inch) thick cooked in foil take about 25 minutes.
5. Allow the salmon to become quite cold in the foil parcel, which will help keep it moist and succulent. Do not refrigerate. Unwrap, then strip off the skin from the upper side with great care. Lift on to a serving platter with the foil strips and pull these out from underneath the fish. Garnish the fish with slices of cucumber, dill, parsley or tarragon and lemon slices. Serve with Watercress mayonnaise.

From the left, clockwise: Baked salmon with herbs and cold watercress mayonnaise; Roast beef de luxe; Smoked salmon and dill special; Tropical feast

WATERCRESS MAYONNAISE

1 bunch watercress, leaves washed, dried, and finely chopped
2 egg yolks
salt
freshly ground black pepper
¼ teaspoon English mustard
2 teaspoons herb vinegar
300 ml (½ pint) olive oil or salad oil
1 teaspoon anchovy essence

Preparation time: 10 minutes

1. Combine the watercress with the egg yolks, salt, pepper, mustard and vinegar and whisk thoroughly.
2. Add the oil drop by drop, at first whisking all the time, then slowly adding it in a thin stream, still whisking, until you have a creamy mayonnaise.
3. Add the anchovy essence, taste and adjust the seasoning and serve at once with the cold salmon.

SMØRREBRØD OR SCANDINAVIAN OPEN SANDWICHES

Choose a 450 g (1 lb) white or brown loaf, unsliced about 16 × 7.5 × 7.5 cm (6½ × 3 × 3 inches). Cut into 6 slices lengthways, then trim off the crusts. Serve in any of the following ways or make up your own toppings, depending on what you have available.

SMOKED SALMON AND DILL SPECIAL

Makes 2 slices
4 tablespoons chilled soured cream
½ teaspoon chopped fresh dill
100 g (4 oz) smoked salmon, sliced
1 small onion, peeled and sliced
12 slices cucumber
salt
squeeze of lemon juice
sprigs of dill or watercress to garnish

Preparation time: 15 minutes

1. Mix the soured cream and dill and use to spread over the bread slices.
2. Roll up the slices of smoked salmon into chunky rolls of about 5 cm (2 inches) and lay side by side along the length of the bread.
3. Arrange alternate slices of onion and cucumber to fill the surface of the bread slices.
4. Squeeze the lemon juice over the smoked salmon and sprinkle with salt.
5. Garnish down the centre with dill or watercress and serve.

TROPICAL FEAST

Makes 2 slices
4 tablespoons mayonnaise
finely grated rind of ½ lemon
1 carrot, grated
1 × 425 g (15 oz) can pineapple rings, drained
18 cooked prawns, peeled, thawed if frozen
black olives or capers (optional)
sprigs of coriander, to garnish

Preparation time: 15 minutes

1. Blend the mayonnaise and lemon rind, then spread on the 2 slices of the bread.
2. Cover with the grated carrot, then arrange half the pineapple rings, prawns, black olives or capers on top and garnish with the sprigs of coriander.

ROAST BEEF DE LUXE

Makes 2 slices
4 tablespoons mayonnaise
1-2 tablespoons creamed horseradish
2 slices roast beef, rare
6 mushrooms, rinsed, dried and thinly sliced
2 hard-boiled eggs, sliced
1 × 397 g (14 oz) can artichoke hearts, drained and halved (optional)
spring onion curls, to garnish (page 18)

Preparation time: 15 minutes

1. Spread the bread slices with a mixture of mayonnaise and horseradish.
2. Cut the slices of beef into 5 cm (2 inch) wide strips and fold in half.
3. Arrange the beef and mushrooms in a line lengthways on one half of the bread, then the artichoke hearts, if using, and then egg slices on the other half. Garnish with the spring onion curls.

64

MARINATED FOODS

ESCABÈCHE OF MACKEREL

3 mackerel, about 750 g (1½ lb-1¾ lb), heads and tails
    removed
25 g (1 oz) seasoned flour (page 26)
oil, for frying
100 ml (4 fl oz) dry white wine
100 ml (4 fl oz) olive or corn oil
juice of ½ orange
juice of ½ lemon
salt
pepper
pinch mustard
2 small onions, peeled and finely sliced
4 sweet gherkins, sliced
50 g (2 oz) black and green olives
1 teaspoon coriander seeds, crushed
To garnish:
fresh coriander leaves
slices of lemon

**Preparation time: 15 minutes, plus marinating
overnight
Cooking time: 12 minutes**

An escabèche is a traditional dish of Spanish origin, in
which the fish is lightly fried and then left to marinate
overnight before being served cold.

1. Thoroughly wash, drain and dry the mackerel with
paper towels. Toss the fish in the flour, then fry for
about 6 minutes on each side in hot oil.
2. Carefully fillet the flesh away from the backbone
and any other bones. Do not remove the skin. Place
flesh side uppermost in a shallow dish.
3. To make the marinade, combine the wine, oil,
orange and lemon juices and seasonings.
4. Scatter the onion rings, gherkins and olives over the
fish. Pour over the marinade and leave for 12-24 hours.
5. Garnish with fresh coriander leaves and thin slices
of lemon and eat with crusty bread as a luncheon dish
or starter for dinner.

MEXICAN CEVICHE

Serves 6 as a starter
500 g (1¼ lb) fillets of Dover sole, plaice or mackerel,
    skinned
200 ml (⅓ pint) lemon or lime juice or a mixture of both
    (4-5 lemons)
4-6 tablespoons olive or corn oil
1 tablespoon chopped fresh coriander or parsley
salt
freshly ground black pepper
1 large tomato, peeled and diced
4 spring onions, peeled and chopped
1 red chilli (optional)

Preparation time: 35 minutes, plus marinating

1. Cut the fillets of fish into diagonal strips a fraction
thinner than your little finger.
2. Place the fish in a bowl and pour over the lemon or
lime juice. Cover and chill for 4-24 hours. Occasionally
spoon the juices over the fish. The fish is ready when it
changes to a firmer texture and has a rather white
appearance.
3. Strain off and discard the juice. Toss the fish strips
in the oil, coriander or parsley and salt and pepper to
taste.
4. Mix with the tomato, spring onion and chilli, if
using. Add extra oil if necessary. Taste and adjust the
seasoning.
5. Serve either in scallop shells or ramekin dishes or
in half avocadoes garnished with more coriander or
parsley if liked.

From the top: Mexican ceviche; Escabèche of mackerel

BARBECUED CHICKEN

4 chicken quarters or about 1.5 kg (3 lb) chicken, quartered
Marinade:
1 medium onion, peeled and chopped
1 garlic clove, peeled and crushed
4 tablespoons tomato ketchup
1 tablespoon soy sauce
300 ml (½ pint) dry white wine
2 tablespoons brown sugar
sprigs of fresh herbs, e.g. rosemary, thyme, sage, mint,
  oregano
3 tablespoons oil
salt
freshly ground black pepper

Preparation time: 10 minutes, plus marinating
Cooking time: 45 minutes
Oven: 190°C, 375°F, Gas Mark 5

1. Wipe the chicken quarters with paper towels and, using a sharp knife, slash the flesh 2 or 3 times. This allows the flavours to permeate the meat, which is protected by the skin. Place in a shallow dish, flesh side down.
2. Mix the onion, garlic, ketchup, soy sauce, wine, sugar and some sprigs of herbs.
3. Pour the marinade over the chicken and leave in a cool place for 8-12 hours before cooking, basting occasionally.
4. Season the quarters with salt and pepper and place in an oiled ovenproof dish. Add the oil to the marinade. Spoon the marinade over the meat and cook in a preheated oven for 35 minutes, basting several times.
5. Transfer to a hot grill or barbecue and cook for a further 10 minutes until brown and tender, basting at least twice with the marinating juices.
6. Serve at once with freshly boiled rice or baked jacket potatoes and a salad.

ROAST DUCKLING
WITH ORIENTAL PLUM SAUCE

450 g (1 lb) fresh red plums or 1 × 440 g (15½ oz) can
  plums, stoned
25-50 g (1-2 oz) sugar, if using fresh plums
8-10 tablespoons tamarind juice (see below)
grated rind and juice of 1 orange
¼ teaspoon ground allspice
¼ teaspoon English mustard
1 duckling 1.8 kg (3¾ lb), dressed and without giblets
1 teaspoon cornflour mixed with 2 tablespoons water
salt
fresh watercress, to garnish

**Preparation time: 15 minutes, plus marinating
overnight
Cooking time: 1½ hours
Oven: 180°C, 350°F, Gas Mark 4**

The Oriental plum sauce is made a day in advance.

1. If using fresh plums, cook in a little water together
with the sugar until tender and cool. Remove the
stones and the skins if preferred, from the cooked or
canned fruit, then return to the juice.
2. Combine the tamarind juice, orange rind and juice
with the allspice and mustard. Mix all the ingredients
together and chill in a covered container overnight.
3. The next day, prepare the duckling by lightly prick-
ing the skin all over with a fork. Sprinkle with salt.
Place in a roasting tin and roast in a preheated oven for
1½ hours, basting at intervals.
4. Heat the sauce and simmer for 10-15 minutes.
Add the blended cornflour and boil until slightly
thickened.
5. Cut the duck into 4 portions. Serve each portion
with the sauce and garnished with watercress.

> **To use tamarind:** take a piece of tamarind pulp
> the size of a walnut, cover with 120 ml (4 fl oz)
> warm water, allow to stand for a few minutes,
> then squeeze and strain through a nylon sieve.
> Discard the pulp and use the liquid. To reconsti-
> tute the dried variety, take three or four pieces of
> tamarind and cover with warm water. Allow to
> infuse for 15 minutes, then strain and use the
> liquid. If all else fails, use lime or lemon juice,
> but these are a poor alternative to the real thing.

BRAISED BEEF OR VENISON

Serves 6
1.75 kg (4 lb) top rib or brisket of beef, or shoulder of
  venison
1 quantity cooked marinade (page 78)
225 g (8 oz) belly of pork rashers, rind and bone removed
2 tablespoons oil
75 g (3 oz) butter
2 onions, peeled and chopped
3 carrots, peeled and sliced
1 parsnip, peeled and sliced
2 sticks celery, washed and cut into pieces
salt
freshly ground black pepper
25 g (1 oz) plain flour
2-3 tablespoons redcurrant jelly, warmed
chopped fresh parsley, to garnish

**Preparation time: 30 minutes, plus marinating
(3 days for beef; 2 days for venison)
Cooking time: 3-3½ hours**

Braising is traditionally browning meat in hot fat, then
cooking it slowly, in a covered casserole, with
vegetables and a little liquid. This allows the flavours
of the marinade and vegetables to permeate throughout the meat, as opposed to roasting which is cooking
with radiant heat in an oven or on a spit over an open
flame.

1. Marinate the meat for the prescribed time, then remove and dry on paper towels, reserving the marinade.
2. Cut the belly of pork into pieces. Heat the oil and
half the butter in a large flameproof casserole or pan
and fry the meat to seal on all sides. Lift on to a plate.
Add the vegetables and fry until they begin to soften.
3. Away from the heat, place the joint over the vegetables, strain over the marinade and season with salt
and pepper.
4. Cover and cook gently for 3-3½ hours or until the
meat is tender. Turn the meat once or twice during
cooking, skimming if necessary.
5. Lift on to a serving dish and keep warm. Strain the
stock into a separate pan. Make a beurre manié by
mixing together the remaining butter and flour, then
add to the stock little by little over a gentle heat. Stir
until the sauce thickens slightly.
6. Add the redcurrant jelly and mix well. Taste and
adjust the seasoning. Cut the meat into slices, pour the
sauce over and sprinkle with the parsley. Serve with
freshly boiled potatoes and seasonal vegetables.

From the left, clockwise: Barbecued chicken;
Roast duckling with oriental plum sauce; Braised beef

SILVERSIDE OF BEEF IN MARINADE

Serves 6
1.5 kg (3-3½ lb) rolled silverside of beef
Marinade:
50 ml (2 fl oz) wine vinegar
450 ml (¾ pint) red wine
1 medium onion, peeled and sliced
½ teaspoon black peppercorns, crushed
1 teaspoon juniper berries, crushed
6 whole cloves
bouquet garni (page 6)
2 tablespoons oil
4 carrots, peeled and sliced
2 sticks celery, chopped
salt
freshly ground black pepper
225 g (8 oz) small onions, peeled and left whole
150 ml (¼ pint) stock
25 g (1 oz) butter
25 g (1 oz) plain flour

Preparation time: 35 minutes, plus marinating overnight
Cooking time: 2-2½ hours

1. Wipe the beef and place in a deep ovenproof casserole.
2. To make the marinade, mix the vinegar, wine, onion, peppercorns, juniper berries, cloves and bouquet garni together. Pour over the meat, then leave in a cool place overnight, basting occasionally if possible.
3. Lift the meat from the marinade and dry on paper towels.
4. Heat the oil in a deep flameproof casserole or large pan. Fry the meat on all sides to brown. Lift out and fry the carrots and celery until lightly browned.
5. Return the meat to the pan and pour in the strained marinade. Season well, then bring to the boil. Cover and simmer over a gentle heat for about 2 hours or until the meat is tender.
6. Thirty minutes before serving, plunge the onions into boiling water for 5 minutes. Drain and add to the pan for 20-30 minutes, to complete the cooking time.
7. Lift the meat and onions on to a hot serving dish and keep warm. To make the sauce, strain the juices into a pan discarding the carrots and celery and add the stock.
8. Make a beurre manié by mixing together the butter and flour and whisk it little by little into the juices to thicken the sauce. Season to taste and serve with the beef cut into slices. Accompany with green vegetables and boiled potatoes.

BUFFET TURKEY

Serves 8
1 × 2.75 kg (6½ lb) turkey, dressed weight
Stuffing:
450 g (1 lb) sausage meat
1 small onion, finely chopped
50 g (2 oz) pistachio nuts, roughly chopped
salt
freshly ground black pepper
Marinade and glaze:
50 g (2 oz) butter, melted
1 tablespoon honey
1 tablespoon brown sugar
juice of ½ orange
1 teaspoon salt
2 teaspoons ground ginger
2 teaspoons soy sauce
2 tablespoons dry sherry
watercress, to garnish

Preparation time: 20 minutes, plus marinating and cooling
Cooking time: 3 hours
Oven: 180°C, 350°F, Gas Mark 4

1. Wipe the turkey.
2. To make the stuffing, blend the sausage meat, onion and pistachio nuts together. Season with salt and pepper.
3. Press one-third of the stuffing into the neck of the turkey to make the bird look plump. Secure the skin with skewers or sew up with fine string and a trussing needle. Spoon the remaining stuffing into the body cavity. Place the turkey into an oiled roasting tin.
4. Mix the butter, honey, brown sugar, orange juice, salt and ginger together. Brush the turkey with some of the mixture and leave in a cool place for 1 hour. Repeat and leave for a further hour.
5. Place in a preheated oven and cook for 3 hours. Cover loosely with foil if browning too rapidly. Baste and brush the turkey with the remaining marinade twice during the cooking time. Test to see that the turkey is cooked through.
6. Remove the turkey from the oven and brush with the soy sauce mixed with the sherry. Leave until cool, then cover and allow to become quite cold before serving. Do not serve straight from the refrigerator but allow to return to room temperature.
7. Garnish with lots of watercress. Serve with a mixed bean salad, coleslaw and baked jacket potatoes.

From the top left, clockwise: Roast pork with juniper berries; Buffet turkey; Silverside of beef in marinade

ROAST PORK WITH JUNIPER BERRIES

Serves 10-12
1 leg pork, about 3 kg (7 lb)
4 tablespoons oil
2 tablespoons juniper berries, pounded
2 garlic cloves, peeled and crushed
freshly ground black pepper
2 teaspoons salt
2 oranges

Preparation time: 10 minutes, plus marinating and standing
Cooking time: 4 hours
Oven: 230°C, 450°F, Gas Mark 8;
      180°C, 350°F, Gas Mark 4

1. Wipe the pork, then, using a sharp knife, deeply score the rind and fat at close intervals. Place the meat in a roasting tin and rub all over with half the oil.
2. Mix the juniper berries, garlic, pepper and a little of the salt together, then press between the incisions in the rind. Leave to marinate for about 2-3 hours, then rub in the remaining oil. Sprinkle with the salt.
3. Place in a preheated oven for 30 minutes, then reduce the oven temperature and continue cooking for 3½ hours.
4. Cover the meat with foil on a hot serving dish and stand in a warm place for 10 minutes.
5. Meanwhile, to make the gravy, add 1 teaspoon of grated orange rind and juice from 1½ of the oranges to the juices in the pan and heat thoroughly.
6. Garnish the meat with the remaining half orange cut into slices. Serve the meat carved into thick slices with the gravy, carrots, broccoli and roast potatoes.

CHICKEN CARDAMOM

4 chicken quarters or about 1.5 kg (3 lb) chicken, quartered
1 teaspoon salt
8 green cardamom pods, seeds removed
½ teaspoon fennel seeds
¼-½ teaspoon chilli powder or cayenne pepper
2.5 cm (1 inch) piece of fresh ginger, scraped and sliced
2 garlic cloves, peeled and crushed
150 ml (¼ pint) plain unsweetened yogurt
2-3 tablespoons ghee or melted unsalted butter
1 tablespoon oil
5 cm (2 inch) cinnamon stick
4 whole cloves
1 medium onion, peeled and finely chopped
few strands saffron, soaked in 4 tablespoons hot water
fresh coriander leaves, to garnish

Preparation time: 40 minutes, plus marinating
Cooking time: 50-60 minutes

The cardamom gives a delicious flavour to this chicken recipe. It is a winner for the busy hostess as it requires very little last-minute attention.

1. Wipe the chicken and place in a large ovenproof dish. Rub the salt into the skin of the chicken.
2. Dry fry the cardamom and fennel seeds, then grind to a fine powder. Add the chilli powder or cayenne. Pound the ginger and garlic, then mix with the yogurt and spices. Alternatively, place all the ingredients in a blender or food processor and blend on high speed.
3. Coat the chicken with the yogurt mixture and leave to stand in a cool place for about 3 hours, basting 2 or 3 times with the mixture.
4. Heat the ghee or butter and oil in a large pan or wok and fry the cinnamon and cloves for a few seconds, then add the onions and cook until soft. Add the chicken and all the marinade together with the water from the strained saffron. Turn gently to seal the chicken.
5. Cover and cook gently for about 45 minutes or until the chicken is just tender.
6. Remove the pan from the heat and allow the chicken to stand for 10 minutes in the sauce before serving. Remove the cinnamon stick and cloves if preferred.
7. Transfer to a hot serving plate and garnish with coriander leaves. Serve with freshly boiled rice.

BARBECUED SPARE RIBS

1.5 kg (3 lb) pork spare ribs
Marinade:
1 whole garlic bulb, peeled and crushed
5-6 fresh red chillis or 1-2 teaspoons chilli powder
150 ml (¼ pint) sweet and sour sauce plus 2 teaspoons
    sugar or 150 ml (¼ pint) mango chutney plus
    1 tablespoon sugar
1 teaspoon cornflour
1 teaspoon baking powder
1 teaspoon bicarbonate of soda
2½ tablespoons Chinese rice wine or dry sherry
2 tablespoons light soy sauce
salt
spring onion curls, to garnish (page 18)

Preparation time: 20 minutes, plus marinating
Cooking time: 1-1¼ hours
Oven: 190°C, 375°F, Gas Mark 5

Have finger bowls of water containing a slice of lemon
or a few flower petals, or small towels ready when
your guests have finished eating.

1. Place the spare ribs in a shallow dish.
2. Place the garlic and chillis or chilli powder together
in a blender or food processor. Add the sweet and sour
sauce or the mango chutney, sugar, cornflour, baking
powder, bicarbonate of soda, wine or sherry, soy sauce
and salt to taste. Blend until smooth.
3. Pour the mixture over the spare ribs and leave to
marinate for 4-12 hours. Baste several times during
marinating.
4. Arrange the spare ribs on racks over 2 roasting tins.
Pour a little water into the base of each tin to catch the
drips and to prevent smoking.
5. Roast the ribs in a preheated oven for 1-1¼ hours.
Turn once or twice during cooking.
6. Serve hot garnished with spring onion curls.

COCONUT MARINADE FOR FISH

Makes 10 skewers
750 g (1½ lb) firm fleshed fish, e.g. monkfish, halibut,
    haddock, skinned
Marinade:
300 ml (½ pint) coconut milk (page 9), using 225 g (8 oz)
    desiccated coconut, or 100 g (4 oz) creamed coconut and
    175 g (6 fl oz) water
2 garlic cloves, peeled and crushed
2.5 cm (1 inch) piece of fresh ginger, scraped and sliced
1 small onion, peeled
few fresh coriander leaves
½ teaspoon chilli powder
½ teaspoon ground turmeric
100 g (4 oz) button mushrooms, rinsed, drained and dried
½ red pepper, cored, seeded and cut into wide strips
½ green pepper, cored, seeded and cut into wide strips
salt
oil, for brushing
25 g (1 oz) roasted peanuts, ground (optional)
wedges of lemon, to garnish

Preparation time: 40 minutes, plus marinating
Cooking time: 8-10 minutes

The fish and delicate coconut marinade complement
each other well and the colours of red, green and yellow are pleasing, too. If you cannot get monkfish,
select thick cutlets of halibut or fillets of haddock, so
that the chunky pieces will stay on the skewers during
cooking. Use wooden or bamboo skewers which
should be soaked in water whilst the fish is marinating. This prevents them burning during cooking.

1. Cut the fish into neat 2.5 cm (1 inch) cubes.
2. Prepare the coconut milk. Pound the garlic, ginger,
onion and some of the coriander leaves to a paste, or liquidize in a blender. Add the chilli, turmeric and coconut milk.
3. Pour over the cubes of fish and leave to marinate for
about 2 hours.
4. Thread the fish, mushrooms and peppers on to the
skewers. Season with salt and brush with a little oil.
Cook for about 8-10 minutes on a barbecue or under a
hot grill, turning frequently.
5. Just before serving sprinkle the fish on the skewers
with the ground peanuts, if liked. Garnish with coriander leaves and wedges of lemon to squeeze on to the
fish. Serve with boiled rice.

From the top: Chicken cardamom; Barbecued spare ribs;
Coconut marinade for fish

HERRINGS IN SOUR CREAM WITH CELERIAC

8 salt herring fillets
juice of 1 large lemon
300 ml (½ pint) soured cream
1-2 tablespoons creamed horseradish
225 g (8 oz) celeriac, peeled, sliced and cut into matchstick strips or grated in the food processor
2 tablespoons chopped fresh chives
salt
freshly ground black pepper
4 tomatoes, peeled and sliced, to garnish

Preparation time: 25 minutes, plus soaking overnight and marinating

1. Soak the herring fillets in a mixture of milk and water for 24 hours. Drain. Cut into strips.
2. Place in a shallow dish and cover with the lemon juice. Cover and marinate for 2-3 hours.
3. Blend the soured cream, horseradish, most of the celeriac, chives, and salt and pepper together.
4. Drain the herring fillets, mixed with the soured cream and celeriac, then turn into a serving dish. Surround with tomato slices and the remaining celeriac and garnish with the remaining chives.

SMOKED MACKEREL AND MUSHROOMS IN HORSERADISH SAUCE

1 smoked mackerel, about 400 g (14 oz)
100 g (4 oz) button mushrooms, rinsed, dried and sliced
1 teaspoon mustard seeds
4-6 spring onions, peeled and chopped
3 tablespoons creamed horseradish
150 ml (¼ pint) single or whipping cream
150 ml (¼ pint) plain unsweetened yogurt
a little salt
freshly ground black pepper
few lettuce leaves, to serve

Preparation time: 45 minutes, plus marinating

1. Skin the fish, remove any bones and discard. Flake the fish into a bowl. Add the finely sliced mushrooms, together with most of the mustard seeds and spring onions, reserving a little of these for the garnish.
2. Stir the creamed horseradish into the cream until smooth. Add the yogurt, with salt and pepper to taste.
3. Pour over the fish mixture, turn gently, then cover and chill for 2-3 hours. Turn into a lettuce-lined bowl and garnish with the remaining spring onions and mustard seeds.

GRAVLAX WITH MUSTARD AND DILL MAYONNAISE

Serves 6-8

1 kg (2¼ lb) fresh salmon, middle cut
6 tablespoons chopped fresh dill or 15 g (½ oz) dill weed
25 g (1 oz) sea salt
25 g (1 oz) caster sugar
1 tablespoon black peppercorns, crushed

To garnish:

2-4 hard-boiled eggs (optional), halved
1 tablespoon lump fish caviar
few sprigs of fresh dill

Mustard and dill mayonnaise:

4 tablespoons French mustard
1 teaspoon English mustard
25 g (1 oz) caster sugar
2 tablespoons herb vinegar
4 fl oz olive or salad oil
3 tablespoons chopped fresh dill, or 1½ tablespoons dill weed

Preparation time: 25 minutes, plus 3-4 days marinating

Buy the salmon 3-4 days before you plan to serve it. The salmon is marinated not cooked and is served in thin slices like smoked salmon. It is well worth searching for the fresh dill which makes this a very special occasion dish. Keep some of the stems of dill for the garnish and mayonnaise in a jar of water with a plastic bag placed over the top positioned low down in the refrigerator until required. This keeps any herb fresh for days. If using dill weed make the mayonnaise in advance so that the flavour improves on standing. Any left over mayonnaise can be kept in the refrigerator. Whisk again before serving.

1. Carefully remove the backbone from the salmon by filleting the flesh close to the bone on each side or ask the fishmonger to do this for you. You will now have 2 identical pieces of fish.
2. Place 1 fillet skin side down in a deep dish or 4 litre (7 pint) ice cream container.
3. Scatter the salmon with the chopped dill, salt, sugar and peppercorns. Cover with the second fillet, skin side up, and a layer of foil.
4. Weight the fish down with a plate and several 1 kg (2 lb) cans of fruit or a clean brick wrapped in foil.
5. Turn and baste the fish morning and evening for at least 3 days and up to 4 days, replacing the foil and weights each time.
6. Lightly rinse then dry each fillet with paper towels. Using a sharp knife cut into very thin slices and arrange attractively on a serving platter, garnished with halves of hard-boiled egg, caviar and generous sprigs of dill.
7. To make the mayonnaise, blend the French and English mustards together with the sugar and vinegar in a small deep bowl.
8. Using a wire whisk, slowly beat in the oil until it forms a thick sauce then add the chopped reserved dill. Cover closely with cling film until required.
9. Serve with a cucumber salad and home made bread.

From the left: Gravlax with mustard and dill mayonnaise; Smoked mackerel and mushrooms in horseradish sauce

PORK PÂTÉ IN BRANDY MARINADE

Serves 8
225 g (8 oz) pigs' liver
85 ml (3 fl oz) milk
450 g (1 lb) belly of pork, rind and bone removed
450 g (1 lb) back bacon with fat, rinded
50 g (2 oz) butter
1 medium onion, peeled and finely chopped
2 tablespoons cornflour
2 tablespoons brandy
120 ml (4 fl oz) dry white wine
2 eggs, beaten
4 garlic cloves, peeled and crushed
1 tablespoon juniper berries, crushed
finely grated rind of ½ orange
salt
freshly ground black pepper
8 rashers streaky bacon, rinded
To garnish:
½ orange
watercress

Preparation time: 45 minutes, plus soaking and marinating
Cooking time: 1½-2 hours
Oven: 160°C, 325°F, Gas Mark 3

Soaking the pigs' liver in milk eliminates the strong flavour, which otherwise would predominate.

1. Soak the pigs' liver in the milk for 4-5 hours.
2. Mince the belly of pork and fat bacon together. Drain the liver, then mince separately and reserve.
3. Heat the butter and fry the onion without colouring until soft. Cool and add to the minced pork and bacon.
4. Blend the cornflour to a paste with the brandy and stir into the meats together with the white wine, beaten eggs, garlic, juniper berries and orange rind. Season to taste and leave to marinate for 2-3 hours.
5. Add the minced liver and mix well. Grease and line a 750 ml (1¼ pint) pâté dish with the bacon.
6. Spoon the pâté mixture into the prepared dish, smooth the top, cover with foil or a lid and place in a roasting tin half filled with warm water.
7. Cook in a preheated oven for about 1½-2 hours, depending on the depth of the dish. When cooked, a skewer inserted into the pâté should come out very hot and the pâté should be shrinking from the sides.
8. Leave the pâté to cool in the dish, covered with a plate and a weight set on top.
9. Turn out and garnish with thin slices of orange and watercress and serve with bread.

CAULIFLOWER, PEPPER AND LEEK GREEK STYLE

½ cauliflower, broken into florets, about 450 g (1 lb)
1 red pepper, cored, seeded and cut into strips
1 green pepper, cored, seeded and cut into strips
225 g (8 oz) leeks
12 black olives
300 ml (½ pint) water
300 ml (½ pint) dry white wine
4-6 tablespoons oil
½ teaspoon salt
few black peppercorns, crushed
1 teaspoon coriander seeds
½ teaspoon fennel seeds
2-3 bay leaves
1 sprig each of thyme, parsley, marjoram or oregano
a few finely chopped fresh herbs, to garnish

Preparation time: 25 minutes, plus chilling
Cooking time: 20 minutes

1. Wash the cauliflower thoroughly and reserve with the pepper strips in a separate dish.
2. Wash the leeks, then trim off the roots and cut diagonally into chunky pieces. Wash again, making sure that all the grit is removed. Drain well.
3. Heat the water, wine, oil, salt and peppercorns in a pan. Tie the coriander, fennel, bay leaves and herbs in a piece of muslin and add to the pan.
4. Place the cauliflower in the pan and cook for 5-10 minutes until just cooked, but still with a bite. Lift out with a slotted draining spoon into a bowl and cool.
5. Cook the peppers in the pan for 2-3 minutes only and add to the cauliflower.
6. Finally, cook the leeks for 5 minutes, then pour the leeks and liquid over the other vegetables. Add the olives and cool. Cover and chill for several hours.
7. Discard the muslin bag, then lift the vegetables and a little of the liquid into 4 serving dishes. Sprinkle with fresh herbs and eat with fresh bread, such as the Onion and parsley party loaf (page 38).

From the top left, clockwise: Bacon chops with sherry;
Pork pâté in brandy marinade; Cauliflower, pepper and leek Greek style

BACON CHOPS WITH SHERRY

4 tendersweet bacon chops, about 100 g (4 oz) each
300 ml (½ pint) medium dry sherry
4 bay leaves
freshly ground black pepper
25 g (1 oz) butter
4 tablespoons redcurrant jelly
2 teaspoons French mustard
salt
sprigs of parsley, to garnish

Preparation time: 5 minutes, plus marinating
Cooking time: 15-20 minutes

1. Place the bacon chops in a shallow glazed or glass dish. Pour over the sherry, add the bay leaves and black pepper.
2. Leave to marinate for at least 1 hour, then lift out the chops and reserve the marinade.
3. Heat the butter in a frying pan and fry the chops on both sides. Pour in the marinade and cook over a gentle heat until half the sherry has evaporated and the bacon chops are tender.
4. Transfer the chops to a hot serving dish. Whisk the redcurrant jelly, mustard and salt to taste into the remaining sherry in the pan. When smooth, pour over the chops and garnish with the sprigs of parsley.

MARINATED AND ROAST LEG OF LAMB OR PORK

Serves 8
2 kg (4½ lb) leg of lamb or pork
1 quantity cooked marinade (page 78)
4 carrots, peeled and sliced
3 onions, peeled and sliced
3 tablespoons oil
salt
25 g (1 oz) flour
450 ml (¾ pint) stock or water from cooking the vegetables
4 tablespoons redcurrant jelly, warmed

Preparation time: 30 minutes, plus 3 days marinating
Cooking time: 2½ hours
Oven: 230°C, 450°F, Gas Mark 8;
      180°C, 350°F, Gas Mark 4

1. Remove the rind from the pork joint if using and score the fat, or ask the butcher to do this for you. Wipe the meat and soak in the prepared marinade for 3 days.
2. Lift the joint from the marinade. Toss the vegetables in half the oil in a roasting tin and season with salt.
3. Lay the meat on top. Brush with the remaining oil and cook in a preheated oven for 20 minutes. Baste with some of the strained marinade, then reduce the oven temperature. Cook for a further 2 hours or until tender, basting once more during that time.
4. Remove the meat and keep hot. To make the gravy, skim excess oil, pour the juices into a pan and stir in the flour. Stirring continuously, cook for 30 seconds. Gradually add the marinade and stock, then whisk in the redcurrant jelly. Taste and adjust the seasoning.
5. Serve with roast potatoes, seasonal vegetables and the carrot and onion from the roasting tin, if liked.

> A marinade is a mixture of ingredients often containing wine or lemon juice in which meat, poultry or fish is soaked for a period before cooking. The wine or lemon juice act as tenderizing agents. If oil is added to the marinade, it is used to baste the food whilst cooking.
>
> For centuries, a marinade was the accepted way of rendering meat more tender. Now the accent is put on taste as well, so many herbs and spices are added to the marinade.

MARINATED LAMB AND SAUSAGE BARBECUE

Serves 6
6 lamb chump chops about 150-175 g (5-6 oz) each
12 large sausages
200 ml (⅓ pint) dry white wine
2 tablespoons olive or cooking oil
2 garlic cloves, peeled and crushed
2 tablespoons mango chutney
1 tablespoon hot or mild curry powder (page 16)
2 tablespoons brown sugar
few sprigs of rosemary
salt
freshly ground black pepper
sprigs of parsley, to garnish

Preparation time: 10 minutes, plus marinating
Cooking time: 12-14 minutes

1. Place the chops and sausages in a shallow dish and prick the sausages with a fork. Blend the wine, olive oil and garlic together, then stir in the mango chutney, curry powder and sugar.
2. Sprinkle the lamb and sausages with a few sprigs of the rosemary. Keep the rest to throw on the embers or on the grill pan whilst cooking. Pour the marinade over the meats and leave for 3 hours.
3. Lift the meats from the marinade. Season with salt and pepper to taste and cook over charcoal or under a hot grill. Baste the meat with the marinade during cooking and turn when necessary.
4. Garnish with sprigs of parsley and serve very hot with baked jacket potatoes and a selection of salads.

TALATOURI

1 cucumber
salt
1 small onion, peeled
150 ml (¼ pint) plain unsweetened yogurt
2 teaspoons chopped fresh mint
2 teaspoons chopped fresh parsley

Preparation time: 5 minutes, plus marinating and chilling

1. Trim the ends from the cucumber. Cut in half and remove the seeds. Sprinkle with salt and leave for 30 minutes. Rinse and dry on paper towels.
2. Coarsely grate the cucumber and onion and squeeze out any excess moisture. Mix with the yogurt, mint and parsley. Season to taste.
3. Cover and chill for 1 hour before serving.
4. Serve with grilled lamb or pork.

MOROCCAN KEBABS

Enough for 16 skewers

750 g (1¾ lb) lean boneless lamb, from the fillet end of leg

2 lambs' kidneys in their suet

Spice marinade:

2 tablespoons cumin seeds, dry fried

2.5 cm (1 inch) piece of fresh ginger, scraped and sliced, or
   1 teaspoon ground ginger

1 medium onion, peeled and sliced

3-4 garlic cloves, peeled and crushed

1-2 red chillis or 1 teaspoon chilli powder

2 tablespoons water

1 teaspoon ground turmeric

3-4 tablespoons chopped fresh parsley

salt

freshly ground black pepper

hot pitta bread, to serve

**Preparation time: 30 minutes, plus marinating
and soaking
Cooking time: 10-12 minutes**

Try these kebabs for a casual lunch or at a barbecue
party slipped into a pocket of hot pitta bread along
with a selection of accompaniments such as radishes,
spring onions and olives. Hand in a paper napkin to
save on the washing up.

1. Cut the meat into 1 cm (½ inch) cubes. Remove the
suet from the kidneys and cut into small pieces. Skin,
core and cut the kidneys into 8 pieces.

2. Pound the dry fried cumin seeds with the fresh
ginger, onion, garlic, chillis and water into a paste in a
blender or food processor. Add the turmeric powder
and parsley and blend again.

3. Mix the meat and suet with the spice mixture and
leave to stand for at least 2 hours. Soak 16 long wooden
or bamboo skewers in water whilst the meat is marinating. Alternatively use metal skewers.

4. Thread the meat, kidneys and the suet pieces on to
the skewers and place under a hot grill for 10-12
minutes or until cooked. Turn frequently and brush
with oil if necessary.

5. Just before the end of the cooking, season with salt
and pepper. Serve with pitta bread and the suggested
accompaniments.

From the top: Marinated lamb and sausage barbecue;
Talatouri; Moroccan kebabs

SALMON AND SCALLOPS WITH TARAMASALATA SAUCE

Serves 8 as a starter
450 g (1 lb) fresh salmon, monkfish or other firm-textured fish
225 g (8 oz) Queen scallops, thawed and dried
175 ml (6 fl oz) dry white wine
85 ml (3 fl oz) walnut or olive oil
1 small onion, peeled and sliced
1 garlic clove, peeled and crushed
juice of ½ orange
juice of ½ large lemon
salt
pepper
Taramasalata sauce:
100 g (4 oz) smoked cod's roe
1 teaspoon lemon juice
2 tablespoons grated onion
150 ml (¼ pint) whipping cream
freshly ground black pepper
2 teaspoons chopped fresh chives, to garnish

Preparation time: 30 minutes, plus 3-4 days marinating

1. Skin the fish and remove any bones. Cut into small strips and place in a shallow dish with the scallops.
2. Mix the wine, oil, onion, garlic, orange and lemon juice and pour over the fish. Cover and chill. Spoon the marinade over the fish from time to time during the next 4 hours and marinate up to 3-4 days.
3. To make the sauce, skin the cod's roe. Place in a food processor with the lemon juice and onion. Blend whilst slowly adding the cream. Season with pepper.
4. Drain the fish and serve. Serve with taramasalata sauce in a separate dish to spoon over the top of each helping, or serve in halved and stoned avocadoes as a starter. Sprinkle with the chopped chives.

SIMPLE MARINADE FOR FISH FILLETS OR WHITE MEAT

4 fish fillets, chicken breasts, turkey or veal escalopes
Marinade:
1 egg, beaten
a little finely grated lemon rind
1 teaspoon lemon juice
1 teaspoon finely chopped fresh parsley or tarragon
1 tablespoon oil
salt
freshly ground black pepper
50 g (2 oz) fresh breadcrumbs, for coating
butter and oil, for frying

COOKED WINE MARINADE FOR BEEF, LAMB, PORK OR GAME JOINTS

3-4 tablespoons oil
1 onion, peeled and chopped
1 carrot, peeled and sliced
2 sticks celery, washed and cut into pieces
2-3 garlic cloves, peeled and crushed
600 ml (1 pint) red or dry white wine
150 ml (¼ pint) wine vinegar
1 tablespoon juniper berries, crushed
1 tablespoon coriander seeds, crushed or 1 tablespoon ground coriander
1 teaspoon black peppercorns, crushed
1-2 teaspoons salt
3 bay leaves
few sprigs of rosemary, thyme and parsley

Preparation time: 20 minutes
Cooking time: 25 minutes

1. Heat the oil in a pan and fry the onion, carrot, celery and garlic until lightly browned. Add the wine and vinegar, juniper, coriander and black peppercorns.
2. Add salt to taste, bay leaves and a few sprigs of herbs. Bring to the boil and simmer uncovered for 20 minutes. Cool.
3. When cold pour over the leg of lamb, pork, or beef and marinate in a cool place for 3 days, basting twice a day. For venison marinate for 2 days only. After marinating, complete the cooking in either of the following ways. Lamb or pork is best roasted and beef or venison braised.

Preparation time: 10 minutes, plus marinating
Cooking time: turkey or veal: 7 minutes
                   fish: 5-8 minutes
                   chicken: 10 minutes

1. Place the fish or meats in a shallow dish.
2. Mix the beaten egg, lemon juice and rind, herbs, oil, salt and pepper together. Pour over the fish or meat and marinate for 1-2 hours.
3. Lift out using a slotted draining spoon and toss in the breadcrumbs until completely coated.
4. Fry in hot butter and oil until cooked through, crisp and browned all over.

MASTER MARINADE
FOR CHICKEN PIECES

4 chicken quarters or 1.5 kg (3 lb) chicken, quartered
1-2 teaspoons sugar
Marinade:
1 small onion, peeled and finely chopped
1 garlic clove, peeled and crushed
juice of 1 small lemon
300 ml (½ pint) dry white wine
1 tablespoon chopped fresh herbs, e.g. parsley, tarragon,
   thyme, oregano, or 1 teaspoon dried herbs
salt
freshly ground black pepper
50 g (2 oz) butter

Preparation time: 20 minutes, plus marinating
Cooking time: Oven – 35-40 minutes or
**   Grill – 20-25 minutes**
Oven: 200°C, 400°F, Gas Mark 6

1. Using a sharp knife, make some shallow slashes in the chicken skin. Place in a shallow dish and sprinkle the joints with the sugar.
2. Prepare the marinade by mixing the onion, garlic, lemon juice, wine and herbs. Season with salt and pepper. Pour the marinade over the chicken joints and leave for 4-6 hours, basting occasionally.
3. Lift the chicken into a buttered roasting tin and dot with more butter. Reserve the marinade.
4. Cook in a preheated oven until tender, basting with the marinade 2 or 3 times, or cook on a barbecue or under a hot grill for 20-25 minutes turning from time to time.
5. Serve with bread and salads.

Marinated salmon and scallops with taramasalata sauce

INDEX